PRAISE FOR
Steal These Ideas!:
Marketing Secrets That Will Make You a Star
by Steve Cone

"Marketing mavens who treasure their jobs—or better yet, want to move ahead—will find themselves constantly using Cone's incredible cache of **ever-insightful tips and ideas** as their guide to innovation and success."
STEVE FORBES
CEO, Forbes Inc.

"With *Steal These Ideas!*, Steve Cone provides **a clear and no-nonsense guide** for getting it done *now.*"
FAITH POPCORN
Founder and CEO, Faith Popcorn's BrainReserve

"**Loaded with lots of great marketing ideas.** A steal at only $18.95."
AL RIES
Author, *The Origin of Brands*

"I thought I would never need to read another marketing book until I picked up Cone's fun, fast, and fantastic guide that **can help any size business anywhere immediately go from ho-hum to world-class marketing.**"
JON LINEN
Vice Chairman, American Express

"With lots of good information on key marketing topics, Steve Cone breaks down branding issues and delivers them with **a refreshing approach and wry sense of humor**."
CLAIRE ROSENZWEIG, CAE, CPMP
President, Promotion Marketing Association, Inc.

"It's not getting easier out there. So what's one to do? You need the hard-earned lessons provided by campaigns that worked and someone who can extract their secret ingredients. **Steve Cone does all that with a true knowledge of our craft and the no-nonsense approach of someone who knows, understands, and respects consumers.** Does he reveal too much? Yes! Now some of the best secrets in our industry are all in one place for all to see."

DANIEL MOREL

Chairman and CEO, Wunderman

"**Entertaining, informed, accessible**—*Steal These Ideas!* is all that and more. I've been faxing pages to clients with a note saying, 'Hey, read this. It's by someone who learned from the same mistakes you're making and can make it all better.'"

RICHARD LAERMER

CEO, RLM PR, and Author, *Full Frontal PR*

"**This book is filled with practical advice for marketers, and the considerable insight that Steve Cone provides can be used every single day.** The lessons he learned and shares are the culmination of his unique career as a marketing visionary for more than three decades."

ADAM ARON

Chairman/CEO, Vail Resorts (Vail, CO)

STEAL THESE IDEAS!

Also available from
BLOOMBERG PRESS

The Financial Services Marketing Handbook:
Tactics and Techniques That Produce Results
by Evelyn Ehrlich and Duke Fanelli

Full Frontal PR:
Building Buzz About Your Business,
Your Product, or You
by Richard Laermer

A complete list of our titles is available at
www.bloomberg.com/books

STEAL THESE IDEAS!

Marketing Secrets That Will Make You a Star

Steve Cone

BLOOMBERG PRESS

NEW YORK

No part of this book may be reproduced, stored in a retrieval system, or transmitted, in any form or by any means, electronic, mechanical, photocopying, recording, or otherwise, without the prior written permission of the publisher except in the case of brief quotations embodied in critical articles and reviews. For information, please write: Permissions Department, Bloomberg Press, 731 Lexington Avenue, New York, NY 10022, U.S.A. or send an e-mail to press@bloomberg.com.

BLOOMBERG, BLOOMBERG LEGAL, *BLOOMBERG MARKETS*, BLOOMBERG NEWS, BLOOMBERG PRESS, BLOOMBERG PROFESSIONAL, BLOOMBERG RADIO, BLOOMBERG TELEVISION, BLOOMBERG TERMINAL, BLOOMBERG TRADEBOOK, and *BLOOMBERG WEALTH MANAGER* are trademarks and service marks of Bloomberg L.P. All rights reserved.

This publication contains the author's opinions and is designed to provide accurate and authoritative information. It is sold with the understanding that the author, publisher, and Bloomberg L.P. are not engaged in rendering legal, accounting, investment-planning, or other professional advice. The reader should seek the services of a qualified professional for such advice; the author, publisher, and Bloomberg L.P. cannot be held responsible for any loss incurred as a result of specific investments or planning decisions made by the reader.

First edition published 2005
1 3 5 7 9 10 8 6 4 2

Library of Congress Cataloging-in-Publication Data

Cone, Steve
    Steal these ideas! : marketing secrets that will make you a star / Steve Cone.--
1st ed.
        p. cm.
    Summary: "A concise handbook of marketing ideas covering advertising, branding, public relations, direct response, and more, illustrated with examples of brands and successful and unsuccessful ads, written by a marketing executive with nearly 30 years of experience in the field"--Provided by publisher.
    Includes index.
    ISBN 1-57660-191-9 (alk. paper)
    1. Marketing. I. Title.

HF5415.C54738 2005
658.8--dc22   2005016691

For Faye especially, and Cliff.

And, to my father and former
Epsilon colleagues—
where marketing history was made
again and again and again.

Contents

Preface

THERE IS A STORY that has been circulating in New York City for many years about the first time Woody Allen and Arnold Schwarzenegger ever met. Picture a swish cocktail party in Manhattan. As the story goes, Woody walks up to Schwarzenegger, glass in hand, looks up, and says, "Arnold, what would it take for me to look like you?" Without skipping a beat, Arnold replies, "Two generations."

Unlike Woody, you won't have to wait that long for a transformation. What I have put together in this book is almost two generations worth of ideas and practical advice you can pick up in one or two hours. The insights and concepts you will find here are just not taught in college, graduate school, or even on the job. Short chapters make it easy to get through, and I'm confident there's enough wit and wisdom to keep your attention.

What I believe has been lacking in the marketing profession for a long time is a quick read, full of real-world ideas to make you and your company more successful, right away. If you use this book as a marketing tip and idea reference guide now, and for years to come, I have done my job. So don't expect an updated, better-than-ever version.

Have fun, enjoy the stories, rip out pages, learn the techniques, and **steal these ideas**. Remember, this is the secret stuff no one ever teaches and it's just what you need to become a marketing star right now—not in a generation or two!

STEAL THESE IDEAS!

1

Three Hidden Ingredients in Every Winning Marketing Campaign

MARKETING CAMPAIGNS are usually very expensive endeavors, often representing hard-won dollars that must be used effectively. Pressure to create a winning strategy can be enormous. The bad news is that this is not the time to play it safe. The good news is that you can minimize the risk and dramatically increase your chance of hitting the jackpot by following this simple rule:

A successful marketing campaign must have three essential ingredients:

1   excitement
2   news
3   a compelling call to action

These days we are busier than ever, with little time to spare. We're tired. We're focused on the minute-to-minute. We're dealing with logistics, and noise, and traffic. It takes a carefully crafted campaign to make us pay attention to one marketing message versus thousands of others that assault us in the car, on the bus, while watching television, shopping, surfing the net, skimming a magazine, and listening to the radio.

When selling anything to anybody, anywhere in the world, always ask yourself, "Does my ad, brochure, billboard, window display, radio spot—create excitement, generate real news, and provide a reason to STOP everything right now and order the product or service?"

Fundamentally, the job of the marketing professional is to excite the potential buyers, to get them to pay attention to his product or service message and not the other guy's. Most marketing campaigns fail badly in the excitement category, and do even worse in the creation of a compelling call to action.

The whole point of any promotion is to be NOTICED and get a RESPONSE. The marketing industry spends $35 billion a month to grab consumer attention, just in the USA.

Will anyone really pay attention to one more burger ad, one more beautiful older-looking couple seeking financial security by walking hand in hand on a deserted beach, one more gleaming auto isolated on a rain-slicked winding road in Monument Valley?

How can you break out of the pack and hit an emotional bull's-eye that compels your target consumer to single out your brand and respond to your offer? How do you make this happen?

Take a look at the following stellar campaigns, all of which demonstrate the power of integrating marketing excitement, news value, and compelling calls to action.

The Ultimate Help-Wanted Ad

If pressed to pick my all-time favorite ad, it would be one placed by Sir Ernest Shackleton, the famous early-twentieth century polar explorer. In 1913, Shackleton placed a very brief announcement in several London newspapers for volunteers for his upcoming South Pole expedition. He hoped to attract fifty to seventy-five inquiries. Five thousand hearty souls responded to:

MEN WANTED *for Hazardous Journey. Small wages, bitter cold, long months of complete darkness, constant danger, safe return doubtful. Honor and recognition in case of success.*
—Sir Ernest Shackleton

All three elements for promotional success: excitement, news, and a compelling call to action were wrapped up in just twenty-six words. No need to add a single syllable.

The Early Days of *Playboy* Magazine

In the early '50s, when I was 5 or 6, it was impossible to figure out exactly what my dad did at work all day. He was pretty vague about it and as it turned out, with good reason. He was writing some of the very first promotional direct mail letters for Hugh Hefner's then new and struggling publication, *Playboy* magazine.

These letters would be sent to compiled lists of men who subscribed to other men's magazines—which of course made sense. What was a little different was how my dad wrote these letters…from the perspective of a Playboy Bunny. Each mailing included a picture of her in full Bunny regalia. The picture

3

Why Advertise?

Most people believe that advertising dollars should be spent solely to launch a new product or service, build brand awareness, and generate leads. There is nothing wrong with these objectives, but by themselves they present an incomplete picture.

There are six essential reasons to advertise, some of which are not obvious.

● **Motivate your "troops."** Advertising has enormous potential to excite employees and if done well will make them feel proud of the company and themselves. New ads should be previewed internally at various employee gatherings. This will create a buzz and employees will then talk the campaign up with family and friends. Be sure to give each employee a schedule of what media the ads are appearing in, and when.

● **Remind existing customers why they are customers.** Customers need to be reminded what a great company you are to do business with, an idea they would never come up with on their own. By creating awareness and jogging their memory, advertising encourages existing customers to take some action. Most "new" business as a result of general advertising will come from your existing customers.

appeared on the letter, the reply device, and throughout the accompanying brochure which included shots of her other Bunny pals. She even signed her name.

Consequently, millions of American men received letters in the mail from "a real live Playboy Bunny," describing the

- **Generate new leads.** Everyone wants new customers, but prospects need information. Be sure to provide a website or phone number that is very visible. Either give them a mechanism to respond or tell them exactly how and where to buy from you. A deadline always helps.
- **Recruit great people from your competitors.** You can really tell that your advertising hit the mark when competitors' employees contact you about job opportunities and cite your advertising as the reason they did. Although they may not mention the ads, a spike in this kind of activity can often be traced to a successful ad campaign.
- **Garner more positive publicity.** Industry reporters see your ads, too. Chances are you will be asked by many for an interview after the launch of a new campaign. Take advantage of their interest and go out of your way to be cooperative. This can be like a little book tour, with you touting the great work of your company through its advertising.
- **Build the brand.** More awareness is always good. It is just that simple.

scintillating attributes of *Playboy* magazine: great fiction, social commentary, and of course more revealing pictures of her and her friends. This approach was way more successful than if Hugh himself or some other male editor had written the letter—because it was just much more EXCITING!

Rolling Stone Magazine

Back in the '70s, the notorious anti-establishment, self-proclaimed gonzo journalist Hunter S. Thompson was managing editor of *Rolling Stone*. He authored a subscription renewal letter that was completely different from what any other magazine had ever contemplated.

The letter, short and to the point, declared that *Rolling Stone* was Thompson's only legitimate source of income. It went on to say that if you didn't respond, he would be thrown into utter despair and probably wind up in Needles, California, "sucking from a nitric oxide tank down to the bottom death blast of freon, listening to German tourists describe their coyote sightings."

Basically, Thompson threatened the recipient, demanding a response, or else. To underline the warning, the outside envelope featured "I KNOW WHERE YOU LIVE," scrawled in large handwriting across the front. Not your everyday *Time* or *Newsweek* renewal letter, to be sure.

This direct mail subscription effort was a huge success, and *Rolling Stone* used it the entire time Thompson was on the payroll. It was so much fun to read. So different. So Hunter Thompson. So exciting.

Pan American WorldPass and How Last Became First

By the time the late '70s rolled around, the experience of flying had been downgraded from glamorous and elite to mundane, overcrowded, and as torturous as a never-ending bus trip. Yet flights were full of corporate executives and middle managers winging their way across the country and around the world on a regular basis. Working hard, making money, getting ahead, these were not happy travelers.

Although the airlines reveled in their popularity, they were also aware of the growing dissatisfaction of their large bloc of business travelers. In a classic marketing moment, several major airlines decided that their best customers deserved to be singled out and rewarded for frequent travel. And thus, the frequent flyer programs were born.

These programs were really exciting for participants. At last, the airlines made a distinction between the tourist and the trooper. Flying for free and upgrading to first class were the big come-ons and frequent flyers went to great lengths to make sure they stayed abreast of every new perk and bonus mile route. It is important to understand what a big deal the frequent flyer programs were at that time.

Working with a small team at Epsilon Data Management, I helped United Airlines create Mileage Plus, one of the first of these reward scenarios. Several years later, I was fortunate enough to create the last entry of a major airline into this new game: Pan American Airways' WorldPass, the richest of all the frequent flyer programs.

According to airline industry analysts, WorldPass probably contributed to Pan Am's ability to remain in business for an additional decade. This is a story about creating excitement and news value even when you are THE ABSOLUTE LAST business in your sector to recognize your top clients.

By 1981, all the other major U.S. carriers had well-developed frequent flyer programs, and Pan Am was seeing the effect on their bottom line. So what to do? The company was lucky to have a marketing director at the time, Adam Aron, who had natural marketing instincts, flair, and an appreciation of the power of big ideas.

The typical frequent flyer marketing approach was not as generous as it appeared. At that time, the goal was to spend as little as possible to communicate with your business travelers, and to be as restrictive as possible in giving out award travel for miles earned.

Adam had a different idea. His charge to me was to create the most expensive-looking program with the richest award structure. He wanted to leapfrog the competition—all of which had well-established programs and, in most cases, a four- to five-year head start. Since Pan Am was the last to arrive at the dance, Adam was determined his airline would be in the dress that everyone noticed.

The core promise of Pan Am's program was to reward individuals who flew a specific number of miles on an annual basis with a "world pass." This pass was an actual gold-colored plastic card that entitled you and a companion to fly anywhere on Pan Am's extensive worldwide system, first class, free for thirty days.

This strategy was a winner from day one. No other airline even remotely had such an award, nor could any of them match the worldwide route structure that Pan Am was famous for. The effect was immediate. WorldPass electrified passengers, Pan Am employees, and the trade press. Adam's focus on giving the customer something that was truly exciting and "richer" than the competition turned the whole industry inside out and left them scrambling to catch up.

So last-in became first in frequent flyers' minds. The initial direct mail enrollment package sent to 80,000 frequent flyers contained a free round-trip domestic ticket good at any time within the next six months—no blackout dates, no ifs, ands, or buts other than the requirement to enroll in WorldPass.

Response rates to this one letter were more than 50 percent. Probably an all-time high in direct mail history, with the exception of responses to letters from the IRS!

Other Quick Airline Stories about Creating Customer Excitement

American Airlines—When you joined the Admirals Club in the early '70s, you received an oversized certificate done in calligraphy and beautifully framed, asserting your club membership. These were hung in offices with pride and were real status symbols.

Continental Airlines—In the '60s and '70s, the legendary chairman, Robert Six, wrote a letter to the airline's best customers once or twice a year, a letter that often went on for pages. It was so personal, so beautifully written, so candid, that customers not only saved these letters as keepsakes, but they also continued to fly Continental just to stay on the VIP mailing list.

Braniff International—In the late '60s and throughout the '70s, Braniff attracted attention with brightly colored planes, leather seats in all classes, fine dining on bone china, and flight attendants dressed in fashionable Halston outfits. People actually looked forward to boarding a Braniff plane—amazing.

One for the Gipper

In 1983, the Republican Senatorial Committee wanted to end the year with a big fund-raising push to their top 200,000 contributors. At the time, they regularly spent 50 cents a piece on highly personalized computer letters to their donor base.

Given their desire to top previous fund-raising efforts, I convinced them to try something totally different for the year-end appeal: a single but very special letter that would cost roughly $7 in the mail. They agreed, and the end result was a one-letter appeal that raised more net dollars (over $2 million) than their archrival, the Democratic Senatorial Committee, raised in an entire year.

Here's what went into that $7 letter:

a) A mailing envelope made to look like a FedEx overnight package but actually sent express mail via the U.S. Postal Service

b) A two-page fund-raising letter with an embossed gold senatorial seal

c) An 8"x10", four-color, signed photograph of President Ronald Reagan with a personalized message: "Stephen, thanks for all your continuing support. Ronald Reagan"

Yes, that's right—we had 200,000 signed photographs, with a handwritten note to each recipient. President Reagan was otherwise engaged, so the task fell to a group of women at a mail production company in Massachusetts who earned extra money for the job. They were each given a sample of the president's handwriting to copy and executed a very credible facsimile.

What could be more exciting to the Party faithful than to receive a personally signed photograph from the President? They loved the attention and the response rate to this package was over 40 percent, as opposed to a typical response rate of 5 to 10 percent.

Don't Leave Home Without It

Karl Malden served as the public face of American Express Travelers Cheques for twenty-five years—an amazing run for any spokesperson. His Travelers Cheques television ads were a perfect combination of excitement, news, and a compelling call to action. First you would see a thief stealing money from some poor unsuspecting tourist's wallet or beach bag or hotel room. Then Karl would arrive on the scene looking like the cop he played in the famous television series *Streets of San Francisco*. He would look you in the television eye and say, "This could happen to you!" And then the call to action: "Don't let a thief spoil your vacation. Get American Express Travelers Cheques." Little wonder American Express became the leader in this category with 75 percent market share.

Mean Joe Greene

Sometimes simple visuals can create excitement on their own. Coca-Cola came up with an ad juxtaposing a sweet 10-year-old fan with the very large and, on the field purportedly very mean, Joe Greene, defensive tackle for the Pittsburgh Steelers.

Tired after a long game, and with an intimidating scowl on his face, Joe approaches the small boy who holds a large bottle of Coke in his little hand. Joe peers down at the boy who, ignoring the scowl, looks up admiringly. A true fan, he offers Joe his Coke. Joe hesitates for a second, then takes the bottle and guzzles it down in one complete, thirst-quenching act. He hands the bottle back and says with a slow smile, "Thanks, kid." The essence of "Have a Coke and a Smile."

Mr. Whipple

Toilet paper is just not exciting. Yet Charmin managed to create a quirky character plagued by supermarket customers who was instantly memorable.

Pity poor Mr. Whipple, guardian of the Charmin display, who worked so hard to keep the product at its peak. Your attention was grabbed and you watched intently as Mr. Whipple caught the next culprit who squeezed the Charmin.

Mr. Whipple made Charmin seem so soft and enticingly squeezable, you felt as if you had to try some yourself. In the privacy of your own home, without being stalked by Mr. Whipple. Great call to action. A top-rate example of making one product stand out in its category.

Peter Lynch, Lily Tomlin, and Don Rickles

As an industry, financial services relies on the same old stereotypical images year after year in its advertising. We all want financial information and financial security for our families, but we are bored with the lame attempts to gain our attention.

Financial services also suffers from being a low-interest category. If you can't eat it, wear it, drive it, apply it, or play with it, it is of low interest. You never actually see or touch most forms of money and that cash in your pocket really has no character or emotional bond.

If you want further proof of how tough it is to wow consumers with financial services advertising, consider that no financial services company has ever made it into the *Advertising Age* Top 50 Ad Campaigns of All Time list.

As Fidelity Investments head of retail marketing in the late '90s, I was determined to walk away from the usual nondescript industry ad approach and inject large doses of personality into a campaign that would really shake up the business.

Anyone with a dime in the stock market knows who Peter Lynch is. And Peter has always been a major advocate of consumers understanding how to invest wisely. So early in my days at Fidelity, I decided Peter would be the perfect spokesperson for a new campaign. He had never been in any form of advertising before. And Fidelity had never considered using a real person to promote their brand.

But I didn't want Peter to be just another talking head, although there are plenty of creative ways to make one person a powerful spokesman. I decided to go into uncharted territory. Take a serious subject, money management, and create a campaign that would be as entertaining as it would be informative on issues like retirement, portfolio management, and the value of long-term investing.

Enter two terrific actors, both world-class entertainers, Lily Tomlin and Don Rickles, whom I paired one-on-one with Peter in a series of TV spots in 1998 and 1999.

The net effect was immediate. Employees loved this breakthrough approach. They were thrilled that Peter had "gone public" to represent the company and that he had two fascinating personalities to interact with. And of course customers and potential customers loved these ads as well. They were just so different. They were even fun to watch and listen to. People responded in huge numbers on the phone and online every time one of these ads ran.

In Simple Language:
What Is a Brand?
What Makes It Successful?
How Do You Manage It?

BRANDING HAS BEEN AROUND as long as humans have occupied the planet. From the day we are born, we continually compare ourselves to others until the day we die. Even after death, the beat goes on with tombstones and markers to eternally signify what our life represented versus the person buried in the next plot over.

Simply stated, a brand is a recognizable person, place, or thing. Our job as marketers is to create brands that are separate and distinct from similar products or services offered by competitors. It's all about differentiation.

Most brands almost always imply a guarantee of a product or service. Roman marble merchants actually deserve credit for the first brand warranty application. To advertise that marble was totally pure they would tag marble slabs *sine cere,* which eventually became the word "sincerely" in English. In Roman times, it meant without wax, implying the marble you purchased was pure and free from cracks filled in with wax. Merchants who sold marble that was illicitly marked *sine cere* were executed. Fortunately, we are not quite so severe with brand managers today.

All successful, well-known brands are usually described in one or two words. They have achieved such a high level of awareness that you immediately identify what they stand for. A successful brand inspires you to love it, notice it, remember it forever and ever, even hate or fear it.

One of the most recognized and successful brands in the modern age is the American flag. This icon can be summed up in one word: freedom. For the vast majority of liberty-loving people on the planet, it represents what humans live for: free will and a chance to pursue their dreams.

Truly great brands have four qualities in common. They are inspirational, indispensable, dependable, and unique. It is hard for any marketer to deliver on the first two, unless you market a country or a religion. But striving to make your brand dependable and unique is the rallying cry marketers should focus on every waking moment.

Brands are complex and come in varying forms. Some brands are "fuzzy" and mean different things to different people. Politicians are an excellent example of this ambiguity. To some, George W. Bush is visionary, focused, principled, forthright, a champion of freedom. To others he is mindless, dangerous, arrogant, and a bully.

Frank Sinatra, who is hard to describe in a few words, is another example of a brand with complex and sometimes opposing traits. For many years outside his home in Palm Springs, California, there was a big sign that read, "Beware of Dog's Owner." Perhaps that says it all. Sinatra could be nasty, tough, unbending, rigid. He could also be kind, loyal to a fault, considerate. In all endeavors one could say he was passionate. Indisputably one of the best male singers of all time. A truly great actor. An enduring brand, but hard to pin down.

Generally, a brand can be described in just a few words:

NIKE	sports equipment
Coke	cola
Marlboro	cigarettes
BMW	cars with German engineering
Porsche	cars with speed and performance
FedEx	overnight delivery
UPS	package delivery
Schwarzenegger	Terminator/governor
Apple	innovative personal computers
IBM	technology giant
Pentagon	military headquarters
NBC	network television
ESPN	sports channel
Playboy	men's magazine
Paris Hilton	public relations junkie
Britney Spears	sexy trashy singer
The Masters	Holy Grail golf tournament
Four Seasons	top-notch hotels
Motel 6	cheap rooms
Las Vegas	gambling mecca
MIT	techno haven for nerds
Harvard	Ivy all the way

How you differentiate your product or service from all your competitors is the whole focus of successful brand management. Fundamentally, brand building and management is all about the combination of these four marketing elements:

1 a compelling unique selling proposition
2 strong visual brand imagery
3 innovative and reliable products
4 memorable and integrated advertising

Additional information about elements 1, 2, and 4 can be found in later chapters.

Unique Selling Proposition

You must be able to describe in a sentence or two what makes your business tick, what makes it unique, how your employees can fully understand what their best efforts produce and why, and what makes your company special.

A favorite example of a unique selling proposition comes from a dinner I attended several years ago. Seated next to the head of marketing for Harley Davidson Motorcycles, I asked the gentleman why Harley was the premium brand in the world of motorcycles, year after year. He responded,

> "We allow overweight middle-aged white guys to dress up in leather on the weekends and ride a Harley through small towns and villages scaring the hell out of the locals."

That is about as succinct a description of a unique selling proposition as I have ever heard. Make sure you are able to communicate yours as well.

Strong Visual Imagery

Symbols or logos make brands last forever in our brains, a little like shorthand for the brand. At their best they are overpowering and universal, like the Nike swoosh, IBM for International Business Machines, BMW for Bavarian Motor Works. My guess is that most car buyers today don't even think BMW stands for anything other than BMW. Combining their logo with a powerful, elegantly simple tag line, "The Ultimate Driving Machine," BMW consistently comes out on top of the fiercely competitive luxury car segment.

You know you have arrived when your symbol is so strong that nothing else needs to be said. For many years, Shell Oil had the word "Shell" inside its yellow shell logo. The logo became so recognizable that eventually Shell dropped the word—it just wasn't necessary and in fact was redundant.

Innovative and Reliable Products

Without an innovative and reliable product, all the best logo designs and unique selling propositions are for naught. A company must continue to innovate and not sacrifice reliability to stand out in the market place. That's why product development, as an initiative, is so vitally important and generally a key element of any marketing effort.

There are endless examples of product-driven companies. Certainly the auto manufacturers come to mind. Innovation was clearly the case when the first airline shuttle service was started by Eastern Airlines—underlining reliability—something to this day only the shuttle services really deliver.

This is not a book about how to create products. It is about how to market them.

But great marketing cannot overcome a ho-hum product. If you find yourself in a company with a mediocre product, get out before it fails.

Memorable and Integrated Advertising

Most advertising is dull, and sometimes even stupid and insulting. Who can blame people for skipping over commercials, changing radio stations, or leafing past ads in magazines if they are bored? Your goal, as champion of a brand, is to get people's attention and deliver an unforgettable message through every appropriate media opportunity.

Simple as it sounds, the less people have to digest the more likely it is they will remember what they have taken in. Combine brevity with a forceful message and you will have a memorable ad. The group running Lyndon Johnson's presidential campaign in 1964 understood this when they decided to show how foolhardy it would be to vote for his opponent, Barry Goldwater, and created the famous Daisy Ad.

The ad opens with a cute little girl in a field of flowers, picking petals off a daisy and counting 1, 2, 3, 4, 5, 6, 7, 8, 9. The camera closes in on her face, then her eye, which then fills the screen with black. A male voice comes on with a mission control countdown: 10, 9, 8, 7, 6, 5, 4, 3, 2, 1, 0.

A loud boom is heard and a picture of a nuclear explosion fills the screen. LBJ's voice comes on evoking W.H. Auden: "These are the stakes. To make a world in which all of God's children can live, or go into the dark." The mushroom cloud turns into a firestorm and Johnson's voice continues, "We must either love each other or we must die." The screen goes black and white lettering appears: Vote for President Lyndon Johnson on November 3rd. A professional voiceover says, "Vote for President Johnson on November 3rd. The stakes are too high for you to stay at home."

Needless to say, the Goldwater folks were not at all pleased and succeeded in pulling the ad from the airwaves, which just generated more publicity for the ad.

A more contemporary example of memorable advertising is the long-running campaign for Champion Mortgage in the '90s. Targeted at people who need money but have fair to poor credit ratings, Champion made their ads very straightforward, with a hard-hitting message that came right from the top. Their spokesperson, the company founder, ended every commercial with the promise, "When your bank says no, Champion says—YES!" That line and the 800 number were all you needed to know. And the line was everywhere, integrated into all television spots, print ads, brochures, pamphlets, loan statements, tee shirts...you name it.

Always a step ahead and often leaps ahead of their competitors visually, Apple introduced their iPod personal music device in 2001. They created a visually stunning campaign that utilized brilliant techno colors as backdrops to show the product in action on silhouettes of human figures in motion.

No matter who you are, what part of the planet you hail from, what your age, you understand what the iPod is all about the instant you see ads in print or on TV. They are so simple, so visually compelling, you have no choice in the matter—your eye is immediately drawn in. Apple's iPod campaign is a prime example of the power of a minimal message, where visual images tell the product story a million times better than words.

As you can see, brand management need not be complicated or require you to read thick tomes with charts and graphs showing the life of a brand. Branding is not made up of scientific principles, like physics. Successful brand management comprises the four elements described above. If you stay focused on how to excel at each, you and your brand will stand to prosper. Marketing successfully is all about simple ideas brilliantly executed that reinforce your brand message.

How to Create a
Unique Selling Proposition

EVERY COMPANY NEEDS a clearly stated or visually obvious unique selling proposition (USP). It can take the form of a short mission statement, or a tag line that resonates with employees and consumers. Sometimes it can even be just a visual representation of the product or service. A term most ad historians credit to legendary adman Rosser Reeves, a solid USP still remains the best way to differentiate your brand from the competition.

Federal Express is an example of a company so closely aligned with its USP that they really are one and the same. It all started with Fred Smith's brilliant concept, one that his business school professor said would never work. In the mid-1970s, Fred put together a business with a couple of small Falcon jets and a great ad campaign created by Ally &

Gargano: "When it absolutely, positively has to get there overnight." And thus, an enduring USP was born to live on as the Federal Express promise. A few years ago, Federal Express recognized the widespread usage of their shortened name, FedEx, as a verb to indicate overnight shipment of a package or document. The company smartly changed their official name to FedEx to trademark-protect this name.

Notice the 8-ounce glass Coke bottle. That unique shape is one of the most recognizable shapes on earth, with or without the Coca-Cola lettering. Coke OWNS this shape. That's their USP. It conjures up the thought, "Only with Coke can you grab this bottle and quench your thirst." Recognizing the power of their one-of-a-kind bottle design, Coke has put this classic container back on the shelves, included the shape in its advertising, and engineered a major comeback in the competitive world of soda. After all, a soda can is just a soda can.

Probably the most powerful commercial USP of all time belongs to Marlboro, a brand that has maintained a worldwide market share of close to 50 percent. The famous Marlboro cowboy represents positioning that spans more than half a century and evokes a sense of freedom to roam, to be myself, to do what I want when I want. It is the romance of the open range—that cowboy mystique that never waivers, generation after generation, that appeals to women as much as men, and works across all levels of race, income, and nationality.

Marlboro has created such a strong universal image that the cowboy sticks in the minds of consumers, even without ever appearing on a box of cigarettes.

In fact, as the story goes, it was a very conscious decision to leave the cowboy off each box of cigarettes. Since the '50s, when Phillip Morris first launched Marlboro in the United States, the Leo Burnett agency has been promotional stew-

ard of the brand. The launch team, run by agency founder Leo Burnett, decided that it would not be right for smokers to actually crush the cowboy in their hands as they discarded each packet of cigarettes—in a sense crushing the legend and the dream of "free to do as I please" that the cowboy represents. Whether this was a stroke of brilliance or luck, it's hard to argue with the outcome.

BMW's USP is embedded, whenever possible, as part of its logo—The Ultimate Driving Machine. This USP is their consumer promise and the company strives to fulfill it in the design and engineering of their cars. BMW charges a premium price in all their car categories and rarely discounts. They are very fussy about dealer service standards and close

down dealers who do not meet them—unusual in the auto business. BMW gets away with saying that there is no better car on the road—BMW is the ultimate. Loyal customers seem to agree. Can you name another car tag line or promise off the top of your head? I can't either.

Three of My Favorite Unique Selling Propositions

These USP examples are personal favorites and represent a varied lot: a car dealership, cheap rum, and the Episcopal Church.

1 Car dealership sign in Boise, Idaho: "Fairly Reliable Bob's". Fairly Reliable Bob's is the largest car dealer in Idaho and, I am told, by far the most successful. I guess you could say: finally, a car dealer who tells the truth.

2 Myers's Rum ad: "Old and Not Improved". Everything about this Myers's Rum ad is in your face. Clearly the opposite of any other liquor ads, and truly unique.

3   Ad for the Episcopal Church: "In the Church Started by a Man Who Had Six Wives, Forgiveness Goes Without Saying". This print ad ran about ten years ago as one of a series that was created to turn around rapidly falling church attendance. The campaign was

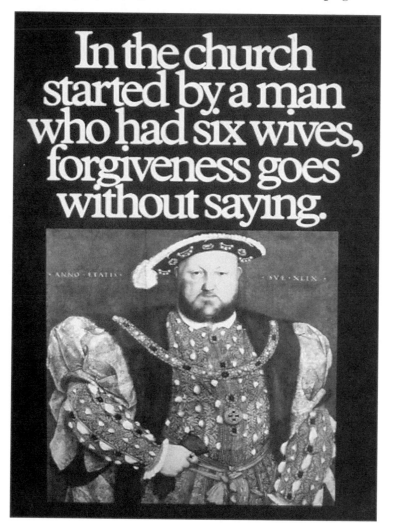

very successful. It was also very controversial with the Church hierarchy and eventually was cancelled for internal political reasons—sometimes reality bites a bit too much?

So, how do you create a compelling unique selling proposition? I promise, this effort is not even close to exact science. It often comes down to one overpowering idea about your product or service that sits there, staring you in the face. Sometimes, it is so obvious that it is difficult to recognize its potential power. You have to step back, gain some perspective, and be honest enough to say—this fact, good or bad, is what my product or service really boils down to.

The best USPs often are discovered by accident. Epiphanies are not planned events and it is important to capture those out-of-the-box thoughts when they occur. No one in the marketing business should be more than an arm's length away from a pen and notepaper. I always carry these tools of the trade when jogging, going to a restaurant, a movie, a wedding, playing a round of golf, et cetera. No matter where I am at bedtime, home or hotel, a pad and pen are handy. Sometimes the best ideas just come to you out of the blue.

Look at your competition and how they position themselves, and then work hard to find a completely different approach. If everyone else is selling cars, you sell service. If lite beer is touted as low-calorie, you sell on great taste. If the competition says how cheap their product is, you might position yours as more expensive and worth every cent.

For a dentist friend (it is always good when your dentist is your friend), I recently came up with a tag line for his practice that is total fact, but something no other dentist ever says out loud: "You Come First. Your Teeth Come Second."

Key Features Only

So you have a great product or service to sell with many nifty features. Pick three of the most compelling and bring them front and center in all your promotional programs.

A long list of features only obfuscates the major reasons someone should buy your product. Long lists tune out the eye and the mind.

Own a car? How many features really mattered to you when you bought it? Probably price, the warranty, and handling.

With many durable products the major feature should focus on ease of use, dependability, and convenience of service—will I get it quickly and at a fair price.

Whatever the product, three major feature highlights are sufficient to give the potential customer enough information to make a serious buy decision.

Bottom line: You need to zero in on a basic product fact and make it come alive as a compelling point of differentiation.

Create, or Hire, or Beg, to Build a Memorable, Distinctive Personality for Your Business

MOST OF THE WORLD'S INHABITANTS look to a personality of some sort to explain their very existence—God, Jesus, Buddha, Mohamed, and all the other major religious figures revered over the centuries. So it should come as no surprise that a distinctive personality can make a significant impact in an advertising strategy.

The personalities featured in tremendously successful campaigns are legion. There are some who created or elevated an existing corporate personality: Colonel Sanders, Dave Thomas, Frank Purdue, Orville Reddenbacher, Chuck Schwab, Peter Lynch. There are others who employed an already well-known face to distinct advantage: Karl Malden, Andy Griffith, James Earl Jones, John Houseman, James Garner, Dinah Shore, Jamie Lee Curtis, O.J. Simpson, and Candice Bergen.

Look at the world of financial services, a category in which all the major players offer very similar products and services. A well-chosen spokesperson can make all the difference. In the early '80s, Smith Barney launched a campaign to build recognition of their brokerage business. They hired John Houseman, a well-known character actor, whose personality exuded confidence and trust, a decision that was as memorable as the campaign they created. In each of the television ads, Mr. Houseman discussed a financial situation that you, the viewer, should be aware of, and then commented on Smith Barney's expertise. He would always sign off with the line: "Smith Barney. They make money the old fashioned way…they earn it."

This series of ads is one of the most successful campaigns of all time. People who were not even alive in the early '80s insist they have seen these television spots and often can repeat the tag line even though it has been off the air almost twenty years. The strength of personality is not to be underestimated.

Another strong example of personality is American Express and their use of Karl Malden, spokesperson on television and in print for the Travelers Cheques division for twenty-five years. This personality/product combination was so compelling that two things happened. First, during the initial years of the campaign, American Express built up and maintained a market share of 75 percent. Second, Karl Malden became known as the spokesperson for *all* of American Express. To the public he was Mr. American Express, even though he had no role in any other American Express advertising. Mr. Malden's persona extended throughout the entire brand by virtue of the power of his personality.

When asked about the use of a spokesperson, my answer is always yes. Why don't more companies do it? Some feel that it will cost too much to pay the individual. Others don't like the idea of a personality selling the product versus the product selling itself. Unfortunately, most products are commodities and need some kind of booster rocket to get them into the consumers' orbit. Personalities can do that, quicker, better, and more persistently than any other promotional device we have at our fingertips.

How to Choose the Right Personality

Choosing a spokesperson can be the single most important factor in a company's quest for better annual bottom-line performance. Whether you hire a celebrity or company employee as your pitch person, you should insist on the following:

1   They genuinely like and understand the product or service being promoted. This point is VERY important. Real interest cannot be easily faked. The best spokespeople are always comfortable with the product or service and show absolutely no hesitation to promote it. If there is a mere hint of "I don't care about this product" from a potential spokesperson, find another as that will show through every time.

2   They are comfortable in social situations, and even enjoy press interviews and employee events. If the person is awkward in group settings, does not care to meet employees on a regular basis, needs two bodyguards to take three steps in any direction, never wants to talk to the press—FORGET about using him. Also, don't expect most people and in particular actors to be good public speakers—they aren't. Ninety-eight percent of us, regardless of our occupation, dread public speaking, interviews, and talking off the cuff. Your potential spokesperson should be willing to get comfortable with the chore of pub-

33

lic speaking. If she is not amenable to being coached in this area—drop her.

3 They are exclusive to your company—no other deals, period. You do not need to hire Tiger Woods because four other companies did. You want someone unique to you—preferably someone who has never done commercial endorsements before and thus is not in any way overexposed.

4 They appeal equally to men and women from ages 8 to 80. Sure, some products are just for women or just for men, but you never know when the other sex might influence a purchase. Kids influence parents and even occasionally, the other way around. Find someone who threatens no particular age group.

5 They must be agreeable to a fully integrated media role. Some people only want to do television and not magazine advertising. Some do not want their images on your Internet site. Others refuse to record radio spots. Any of these "I won't dos" means this person is not for you. In the mid-1990s, when I ran marketing at Key Corp, a large financial services company, I hired Anthony Edwards of *ER* fame to be our spokesperson. He was a huge hit from day one. He fit all of the above criteria and was enthusiastic and cooperative about participating in all of our customer touch points. Here is the list of media applications that Anthony agreed to:

- Television, print, radio, various brochures and pamphlets
- In-branch signage
- Key Corp's Internet site
- The voice of Key Corp's 800 number that customers called for all manner of questions, balance information, product queries, etc.

- The cover of Key Corp's annual report, including a question and answer interview inside
- Regular attendance at analyst meetings and employee-recognition events
- Participation in several press conferences each year

Anthony was a delight to work with and is a poster boy for exactly the way these relationships should work.

Going Hollywood

The very first step in finding a spokesperson other than a company employee is to seek the services of a top-notch commercial agent. Advertising agencies have access to the world of commercial agents and can generally guide you to someone you will be comfortable with. Begin by meeting face-to-face. Do not delegate this chore to your agency. YOU must establish an ongoing relationship with the commercial agent. Any agent worth a commission will want to get to know and be comfortable with you. There must be good personal chemistry and all the parties involved should share your commitment. Without it, the chances of success diminish greatly.

Once you tentatively decide on a personality, both of you should meet and discuss all aspects of the potential relationship. Again, do not discount personal chemistry. If this means you have to fly across the country and stay in Los Angeles for a day or two, make sure it happens. Use the criteria above and you have a very real chance of major success for both sides.

A Word about Voiceovers

The craze today is to hire well-known personalities with pleasing or distinctive voices to narrate television commercials. This is not for the faint of heart. Annual fees range from $50,000 to as high as $1 million. And although big bucks are put down on the table, most marketers do not get the most for their money as they usually limit the voiceover to a single medium… television. The real payoff is a spokesperson who not only appears in your ads but also narrates off-camera. Use his voice on the radio and as your phone-service voice so that his participation in your campaign is truly integrated. Verizon uses James Earl Jones in much this way.

Corporate Mascots

Corporate mascots are actors who portray made-up characters, created exclusively for your company. They are usually unknown to the public until they debut as your company spokesperson. Examples of famous corporate mascots are the Pepperidge Farm man, the Marlboro cowboy, the Maytag Repairman, and Mr. Whipple. Properly positioned, these spokespeople engender interest, loyalty, and even affection.

Today, companies do not go this route as much as they did in earlier decades. Instead, many just use models and unknown actors to pitch products without injecting any personality into the nameless spokesperson. They even forego a polite introduction, such as "This is Anne Smith for Acme household products." As you would expect, this nameless, flat approach is weak and not recommended.

Animated Characters

The advertising world's use of animated characters began in the early days of television with Speedy Alka Seltzer, Mr. Clean, and Aunt Jemima, and expanded to characters like the Jolly Green Giant, Tony the Tiger, Snap, Crackle, and Pop, the Trix Rabbit, and the Keebler Elves. Other than Speedy, this lively group of characters is still in use today, decades after they first arrived on the scene.

Probably the most famous and enduring of all animated characters is the Pillsbury Doughboy. He is worth untold millions in goodwill and really embodies Pillsbury in the minds of consumers worldwide.

Animated characters are the easiest of all spokespeople. They are likeable, do not have attitude, usually avoid getting into personal trouble, and rarely turn off constituents with their political views. Plus, they don't need their own VIP trailers or dressing rooms, cappuccino breaks, or trips on the company jet. But, similar to their human counterparts, they do need contracts, they should be exclusive to a particular company or product, and they require the services of an excellent trademark specialist.

Companies with a serious message beyond biscuits and cereal can also benefit from the use of animation. Metropolitan Life is proof positive of the power of a serious message delivered by cartoon characters—Charlie Brown and his Peanuts gang. Met Life has used the Peanuts characters for twenty years and probably will for another twenty, and beyond. The company is always at the top of the list in recall in insurance company focus groups. And clearly the serious business of insurance is enhanced by this enduring relationship with Charlie Brown and team.

Animals

Using animals has always been a popular way to get consumer attention and affection focused on a particular brand. It's no surprise to anyone that pet food companies use pets as their "spokespeople." Morris the Cat is among the better remembered. But the real question is—what brand was Morris representing? I certainly can't remember. Therein lies the rub.

There is no question that cute puppies or cats or birds or horses that speak English get instant attention and often are remembered fondly for generations. In a 2004 Yahoo! consumer poll of popular advertising icons, in which 600,000 people responded nationwide, the number two choice was the AFLAC Duck.

Here are the top five most popular icons from that survey:

1 M&M Characters
2 AFLAC Duck
3 Mr. Peanut
4 Pillsbury Doughboy
5 Tony the Tiger

Interesting that all but the Duck have peddled their respective products since the '50s and are as popular today as fifty years ago. Which underlines another reason why companies choose to use animated characters or animals— they never grow old and cranky. They never die. They live in a never-never land in our minds.

Back to the rub in the use of live animals like the AFLAC Duck. People love the duck but don't know what AFLAC actually does. At this writing, AFLAC is downplaying the duck in their current advertising in an attempt to better explain the services they provide. So animals can be tricky. The more you can embed them into the actual product or service message, the more likely you can hit the correct balance between cute icon and what you actually do for consumers.

Deceased People

Deceased people work as spokespeople too, but only if the fit is unique, realistic, and done in good taste. And long-gone dead people are way better than the recently departed—think Henry VIII, not Henry Fonda. In general though, this is a tricky category and 95 percent of the time not the right approach to take. That said, there have been a few campaigns over the past twenty-five years in which the use of the deceased has really made a big impact. Probably the best remembered was the long-running IBM effort in the '80s for its line of PCs with a Charlie Chaplin character as spokesperson. Chaplin played an everyman character in his silent films and generated huge appeal as a simple person caught up in a complex world.

The Chaplin character was effective for IBM on several levels, principally because PCs were new to the market. First, it reinforced the notion that a PC was no big deal. You did not have to be a genius to figure it out, in fact anyone could learn to use one. This was an important point to get across in the early days of PC availability. Consumers were wary and didn't want to be stuck with a new-fangled machine that they wouldn't be able to work. Second, the Chaplin character is viewed as simple and frugal, so despite the PC's cost the potential buyer could think, "Gee, I am not really being extravagant by purchasing one." This campaign was truly brilliant and helped the entire PC category take off. It was a perfect fit between a long-dead movie star and modern technology.

How about Fred Astaire and Dirt Devil vacuum cleaners? These ads ran at holiday time for several years in the '90s, and then disappeared. They were cute and clever, but what really is the connection between being light on your feet and cleaning the floor? Well, none. Plus, the image of Astaire with a vacuum cleaner dance partner cheapened the memory of this great performer to millions of his fans. These ads did, however, get Dirt Devil noticed as a brand. Net net, this was not a bad launch strategy for a category with little general appeal.

During the last quarter of 2004, Ford Motor Company began a new campaign for its relaunch of the classic Mustang. Old film clips of Steve McQueen were edited so he appears as a no-nonsense driver of this newly designed retro Mustang. Will this macho film star from the '60s and '70s really connect with the target audience? Perhaps with the 50-and-older crowd. Doubtful with younger potential buyers, but time will tell.

As I stated above, you must be careful with spokespeople who can no longer speak for themselves and have clearly never used the current-day version of the product or service. With the exception of the IBM effort, where a live person imitated Chaplin, showcasing the deceased amounts to shocking people into paying attention to your message. The shock part works, at least with those who remember or have read about the deceased character in question. What this shock leads to could be good, bad, or indifferent for your product. It's definitely risky business.

There is an agency in Los Angeles that specializes in representing famous deceased people through their heirs. This group, The Roger Richman Agency, is the right place to contact if you have any desire to pursue this approach.

But What If My Spokesperson Does Something Really Bad?

I mentioned O.J. Simpson earlier. For many years, he was a very strong and likable personality as Hertz's worldwide spokesperson and did his part to help them remain number one in the rental car industry. Then the murders and the trial. What happened? Hertz acted swiftly and immediately cancelled O.J. and all promotional traces of him. Guess what. No harm done at all, other than the loss of a sterling personality. So don't be afraid to use people just because there is a risk of their image becoming tarnished at some future date. If trouble happens, just move on. Consumers will too.

You Have to Be Able
to See It to Read It

IT SEEMS AS IF there has been a conspiracy among art directors ever since paper was invented to create ads that are impossible to read. First they pick the smallest, hardest-to-read type and then go one size smaller. If that does not make reading hard enough, they will throw in some white reverse type to seal the deal.

You might think of this problem as the "23/63 effect" in which scads of 23-year-old art directors create ads that they fail to remember must be read by scads of 63-year-olds.

Art directors are not evil people and, in fact, they would like their ads to be seen. "Seen" is the operative word here. Their primary focus is on how the ad looks, from a design standpoint. Its readability is not on the radar screen. Art directors waste billions of marketing dollars year after year on "eye tests" that don't work. Yes, billions.

Pick up any magazine and try to read the ads. The vast majority, say 85 to 90 percent, are in sans serif type (type without feet), with typeface so small that your eye really cannot adjust. And of course, you and I make it a point to try to read the ads. Think about the average reader.

When a person picks up a promotional letter or brochure or skims over an ad in a magazine or newspaper, his eye moves at about a hundred miles an hour. What is going to stop the eye dead in its tracks? Certainly a clever headline that is easy to see will slow it down and may even stop it for a split second. In that second the eye scans the rest of the ad and tries to focus on what to read next. If the rest of the ad is in mice type, the likely outcome will be to move on or, in the case of a promotional letter, toss it into the circular file.

Your job is to give your ads EVERY chance of being read and acted on. Small type is the enemy. Sans serif type is the enemy. Reverse type is the enemy. And to not insist on the art director doing your bidding is a cardinal and unforgivable sin.

You don't have to take my word for it. Many studies have been done on type readability. Let me cite just one from the 1995 book by Colin Wheildon, *Type and Layout: How Typography and Design Can Get Your Message Across— Or Get in the Way* (Strathmoor Press): "Body type must be set in serif type if the designer intends it to be read and understood. More than five times as many readers are likely to show good comprehension when a serif body type is used instead of a sans serif body type."

Four Tips to Readability

1 ALWAYS insist on serif type for all your ads—just like every newspaper and mainline magazine on the planet uses in their articles to help the eye connect to the words on the page. This book is printed in serif type. Almost all books are. Serif means that each letter is finished off with a little foot that helps the eye literally finish seeing the letter.

2 IF you absolutely must use sans serif type, apply it to bold headlines only.

3 ALWAYS refuse to use reverse type, which is simply impossible to read. Let your competitors use reverse type all they want. Let them waste their money on ads that have no readability.

4 ALWAYS think of your readers as 55 or older and focus on a type size that is kind to their eyes.

The Good, the Bad, and the Ugly

During the course of several days in late 2004, I randomly selected campaigns in magazines and newspapers to demonstrate how difficult many of today's print ads are to read.

The Good

Bristol-Myers Squibb

This is a powerful campaign. It uses a real American hero, Lance Armstrong, the greatest American cyclist of all time, as its poster boy for Big Pharma's huge impact on saving and

extending human life. The big drug companies are under constant attack from the government, from AARP, from class action lawyers, from...just about everyone. Bristol-Myers Squibb actually strikes back by pointing out the miracles of drug research applied to a compelling human story: Lance successfully battles cancer and comes back to win a record-breaking sixth Tour de France.

Everything works here. The ad tells a story that is hard to resist. The layout is clean and the type very easy to read. Bristol-Myers Squibb has also run TV ads with the same theme. The tag line is a bit hokey but reinforces the message the drug companies need to get out: "We transform lives and eliminate suffering and we're damn good at it." Implied—you are way better off with us than without us. And they are right.

Colors

Red is the most powerful, action-oriented color, period. Think blood, think el toro. You want consumers to take action, right?

As a general rule, avoid using any colors in promotional materials that you see in most bathrooms: beige, light green, and blue.

It doesn't matter how rich or poor or educated or old your target customer is, everyone responds naturally to bright colors. As for financial services, all the talk over the years about how green is a great color because it implies money and red is not because it implies "being in the red" is simply hogwash—whatever color that is.

The best contrast color combination for readability was discovered long ago by Western Union in the heyday of the telegraph and telegram—black letters on a yellow background.

If you never read the rest of this book, just tear out this chapter and tape it to your desk. Follow the advice above and you will dramatically increase the chances of your marketing materials actually getting read.

Premium Brands in Print: Where Less Is More

Premium brands that sell products everyone is familiar with do not need much, if any, explanation. In fact, the objective of these print ads is to make your emotions take over and imagine how swell it would be to wear that Rolex, or buy a beautiful diamond ring for your loved one, or sip some really smooth whiskey.

Oh yes, and these ads want you to decide to pay more, a lot more, for the privilege to own the brand on display. After all, you can buy a perfectly good watch for $100. The cheapest Rolex is around $7,000.

It's hard to top the diamond industry's famous tag line: A Diamond Is Forever. So why even try? In all these print examples, the product is the complete HERO. And the consumers get excited thinking about the possibility of

Every barrel of Jack Daniel's Single Barrel Whiskey is hand-selected by Master Distiller Jimmy Bedford for its unique flavor and character.

[Which is a pretty good reason for you to select it too.]

Please drink responsibly.

49

this hero status rubbing off on them. Notice, no prices and practically no product features in any of these ads—detail would ruin the dream, and premium brands depend first

and foremost on dream fulfillment. The David Yurman watch ads even allow you to associate with cool celebrities, like Ed Burns pictured here.

American Airlines

Here are two ads from a 2004 campaign for American Airlines. One is excellent and one is far from it. The ad with the close-up face shot is visually compelling and points out the major advantage American has over its discount rivals—the chance to ride up front in First Class as a loyal frequent flyer. The other ad is not nearly as powerful. The visual of a near-empty walkway is not remotely believable and it's a very barren kind of set-

ting. The tag line "We Know Why You Fly" is confusing. What exactly does American Airlines know? I just try to get from point A to point B for any number of reasons and flying is the only practical way to do so. Plus, the travel industry and airlines in particular should be careful not to promise more service than they can deliver—namely on-time takeoffs and landings.

So, same airline, same year, but completely different ad approaches. One gets an A and the other a D+.

Thomas Pink—aka PINK

How do you sell really expensive shirts? All image. And if a color is your name by all means show it—the pink vertical strip on the right-hand border is distinctive and just the right

touch. And of course you are supposed to know that Thomas Pink sells shirts in all sorts of colors and cuts and weights. But really, couldn't they stop being so British old school for a minute and show a Web address so at least I could figure out where the U.S. stores are located?

Vanguard

There is a nice warm feeling to this ad series that just makes you feel good about the fine folks at Vanguard. This particular ad focuses on retirement and the theme of "just leave the

heavy lifting to us." After all, can you do better than Vanguard's collection of no-nonsense money managers? Notice the book visual and Chapter 17 at the top. As I said, I like the warm feeling here—you are all cozy with the book from Vanguard. It also implies they have everything in "their book" you could possibly ever want in terms of mutual fund investments. The stickum is a nice homey touch. How can you resist!

AIG

For most of its history, AIG (American International Group) did virtually no advertising. Then several years ago they embarked on a global brand-building campaign. All their TV and print ads are bare-bones simple with their distinctive blue background and plain AIG logo in reverse white on a one-third page size. The basic pitch is "we are big and just better than everyone else in the insurance business." The big AIG telegraphs that message very effectively. No glitz. No sleight

of hand. No beautiful shots of buildings or conference rooms or people in them. We just do what we do and you should damn well pay attention. Quite effective.

New York Times

And you thought the *New York Times* was just a bunch of faceless far-left reporters churning out all manner of global news generally fit to print. Of course only this news organization has the ego to package a guide to all the essential knowledge you

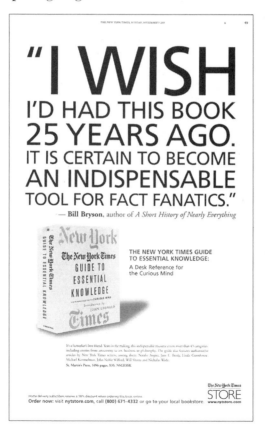

ever need to know. But this ad proves the *New York Times* can create a layout superior to 98 percent of the companies that place ads in its pages. Headline is great. Makes you say, "Yeah, I wish I did!"

Bose

Bose does straightforward ads in black and white. There is a lot of copy if you choose to read it but you can get the whole story with just a glance at the subheads. Nothing flashy for this sound equipment company. They don't have to shout. They are comfortable just stating the facts. You want to buy? Plenty

of ways to respond and to find out the price—which is exactly the action these ads compel you to take.

The Bad

This next batch of four ads is not horrible, but each ad has flaws that prevent the readership that might otherwise be there.

Shell

One has to come to the conclusion that art directors have never heard of serif type.

This corporate ad for Shell has a nice story of cleaner fuel days in the planet's future, but the top of the ad is too visually busy for the eye to really pay attention. The headline is readable with white reverse type on a plain black background, but here the eye has trouble adjusting to too many different type sizes bunched so close together.

The body copy is clean, certainly readable compared to the "Ugly" ads below, but serif type would greatly improve the chances of it being read.

Cadillac

This ad is a two-page affair—the technical term is a "spread." On the left side you see a beautiful silver Caddy on a black background, a pleasing visual with a look that really has some "legs." Unfortunately, the body copy on the right side does not compel you to stay with the ad.

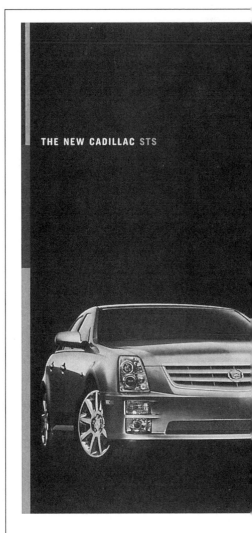

THE NEW CADILLAC STS

Not to be too nit-picky, but the headline is awkward and just plain bad English. The key points here are that you get precision handling and a fluid ride. Why doesn't it just say so

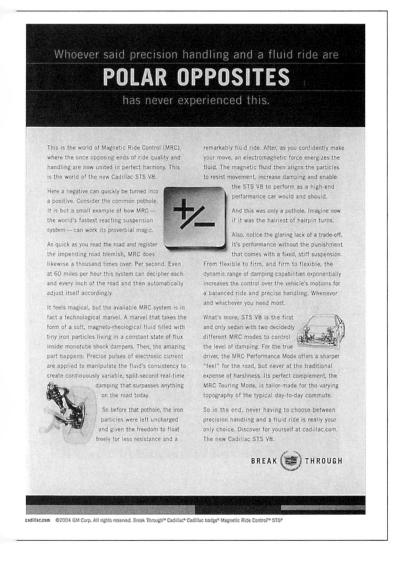

in a much larger type size that the average Caddy customer might be able to read? And of course, do away with the sans serif type.

TD Waterhouse

Finally, an ad with serif type in the body copy. Decent headline, easy to read. So what's wrong? For starters, this layout has been used a million times and just doesn't stop me in my tracks. Plus, who is this guy? Sure, if you watch *Law & Order* all the time, you are familiar with the face of actor Sam Waterston. The problem is this spokesperson is not

connected to the rest of the ad. He just stares at you sort of letting you know he is being paid…to stare at you.

Patek Philippe

Leave it to the Swiss to attempt to sell you a $25,000 watch by claiming your heirs deserve it more than you. But fine—it is hard for watch companies to differentiate themselves and Patek has claimed a niche and is sticking with it. The type is fairly readable and clean in black on a white background. This ad just doesn't go far enough. I'd like to know why they think my watch might last for 200 years. Are there any facts that back

up their generational claim? This ad needs to tell a story, not just lay out a tag line with a huge promise of immortality and move on.

Just Ugly

Putnam Investments

This ad that appeared in the *Wall Street Journal* is a joke, right? Try to read it if you can. The picture of the founder on the left is easy enough on the eye, assuming you care enough to look, but then, the entire right-hand side of the ad is 100 percent IMPOSSIBLE to read. I can't even tell if the body copy is supposed to be read horizontally or vertically. And, I don't care. This ad almost wins the award for least able to read. Except, there is always another that is even worse.

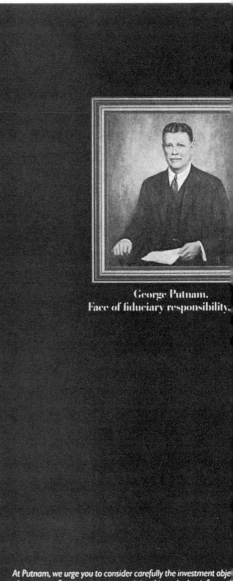

George Putnam.
Face of fiduciary responsibility.

At Putnam, we urge you to consider carefully the investment obje
plan sponsor for a prospectus containing this and other informati

Ed Haldeman.
Face of fiduciary responsibility, 2004.

Ed Haldeman, our new CEO, comes to absolute priority. Under his leadership, we're
work each day with just one overriding creating one of the strongest fiduciary cultures
mission: doing what's right for the investor. In the mutual fund industry. Ed believes in
"We have a responsibility to manage money as hard work, high standards, and the pursuit
if it were our own" is not just his credo, but his of long-term performance for one reason. You.

PUTNAM INVESTMENTS

and fees for any fund. Ask your financial advisor or
before you invest.

| Not FDIC Insured | May Lose Value | No Bank Guarantee |

© Putnam Retail Management 2004

65

Barclays Global Investors

The Grand Slam No Way It Can Ever Be Read Award goes to this ad. There isn't really anything else that needs to be said.

The Truly Ugly

Let's start with the November 15th, 2004, issue of *Business-Week* magazine. I discovered four different single-page ads, one right after the other, that are virtually impossible to figure out and to read.

1 Archer Daniels Midland. The visual is strange enough with the well-groomed child, spoon in hand, who is supposed to be…what? Thankful, hungry, mindless, not happy with corn-flakes again for breakfast? But the reader would never stop

to read the ad to figure it out. The white reverse body copy is an eye test not worth taking. And who the heck is this ad from? If you really, really look hard at the bottom right you see ADM—which means absolutely nothing to 99.9 percent of America.

2 Samsung. This ad is just bizarre. There is no place for the eye to center on, just a jumbled collection of images that make no sense. You might notice the headline: Sculpted by Samsung. You have no idea what the visual next to it is trying to convey. And the white reverse body copy in the lower right will never get more than a split-second glance.

3 Siemens. Wow, a bunch of business types hanging around a conference table, now that's a visual that is just going to… let me pass it by at a million miles a second! And to top it off, even if for some unknown reason I actually tried to read the body copy, I'd need a magnifying glass to do so—perhaps from a German optics company!

4   UPS. I am surprised here because UPS, in general, does an excellent job of visually promoting its brand and services. The headline here is okay, but the whole ad is way too busy and there is that white reverse type again—which makes reading a chore and therefore will find little readership.

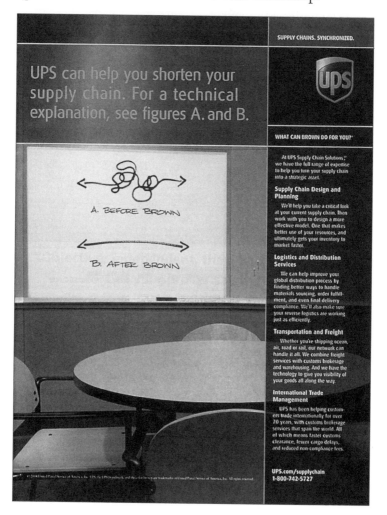

Brochures Kill Trees:
Make the Trees
That Die for You Count

BROCHURES, which take the most time to create, also have the least likelihood of ever being read by their targeted audience. You can dramatically increase readership by following the four tips in the last chapter plus these six suggestions:

1   Put a picture of a person on the brochure cover along with what are called knock outs. Knock outs are quick, one- or two-line highlights of the contents within. The person on your cover can be your spokesperson, your boss, a customer, or an expert in your company's field. Whomever you choose should be highlighted within the brochure as well, perhaps in an interview format.

2   On the front inside cover, summarize the key takeaways of the brochure in bold and easy-to-read copy. After all, why force the readers to go through the whole document to determine their interest? Give them the basic pitch right up front. This way you stand a much better chance of their reading enough to make a decision, as opposed to putting the brochure aside "for when they have more time"—a time that often never happens.

3 Tell the readers what you want them to do—on every page. Call us at this toll-free number and/or visit us at the following website....

4 Regularly use a question and answer format within your brochures. For a century, psychologists have said that people see questions and subconsciously want to read the answers. Who are we to argue with the human psyche?

5 Have a real contact name and return address prominently displayed, preferably on the back cover.

6 When potential readers grab your brochure, they will make split-second decisions about whether to read or toss it. How do you stop them in their tracks and prevent that trash can lob? Always keep this thought at the top of your mind when designing a brochure. Think and act like you are the weekly layout editor of *People* magazine. And while you are at it, subscribe to *People* so that you get a weekly reminder of what "the folks out there" really like to read.

A word about photography and artwork. Most brochures contain abstract art or pictures of people, places, or things that have no bearing on the topic at hand. This stuff is often just filler that supposedly generates enough interest for the reader to thumb through the brochure to its conclusion. AVOID this approach. It has the opposite effect.

As a general rule, do not fill your brochure with random artwork unless you are in the fine arts business. And make sure your photography focuses only on people or surroundings that are part of the story.

Consider a brochure as a short magazine and do what great journalists and news photographers do. Copy these professionals faithfully in the creation and execution of your promotional materials. The pictures you use have to be an integral part of your story. Think what will make a potential reader pick it up with the same curiosity and anticipation that popular magazines generate with their fans.

The same principles apply to annual reports. Thousands of annuals are produced each year for companies and charities. Most get little more than a glance on the 100 mph trip from the inbox to the file drawer or trash bin. There is simply no reason for this fate. Why not make your annual interesting to see and read? Think...short magazine.

When I was head of marketing at Key Corp, I put our spokesperson, Anthony Edwards of *ER* fame, on the cover of our annual one year, and Chuck Schwab the following year. In each case they were interviewed in a special section inside. Anthony on how he saw his role of spokesperson as helping families get a grip on their finances. Chuck on the power of combining the resources of Schwab and Key Corp to provide terrific investment options for Key Corp's customers around the nation.

Annual reports can even generate cash. Take advantage of this yearly communications bonus and include a promotional section of some kind with a special offer for shareholders. They will appreciate your effort to showcase an item they might want to buy and you will enjoy minimizing the expense of printing the annual as a result of some incremental business.

Who says annual reports must be boring beyond belief? A dull annual telegraphs shareholders or supporters that you really don't care if they read it and consequently you really

There Is a Reason Why *People* Magazine Is the Most Popular Magazine of All Time

Year after year, in good times and bad, *People* magazine always maintains or grows in circulation. What's more, *People* generates the largest number of ad pages of any magazine in the world.

You can translate the success of *People* to your everyday marketing efforts, including brochures and other promotional materials, by utilizing the four simple steps below.

1   Use pictures of real people
2   Use captions, ALWAYS
3   Write concisely; this is not a government report
4   Leave plenty of white space on every page

People magazine uses real people and so should you. Showcase the actual people who run your company, manage the service, or who are customers who agree to be profiled. Avoid using paid models or stock photography of people no one knows.

People always want to know about people.

don't care about them. Let your competitors bore them to death. You can do better, much better.

Hot Magazines

Year after year, surveys taken by *Advertising Age* and other observers of the publishing industry show *People* magazine ranks number one as America's favorite. Here are the top six favorites in the latest available *Advertising Age* survey.

People	56.7%
Maxim	49.6
Entertainment Weekly	48.0
Rolling Stone	42.4
New York magazine	34.0
GQ	32.2

(2003 Ad Age survey conducted by Lightspeed Research)

7

Everlasting Tag Lines

TODAY, MOST TAG LINES OR SLOGANS are platitudes that speak to trust, dedication, partnership, excellence, achievement, Mom, and apple pie. They focus on the business category, or life in general—but not on the company.

Take the financial services industry, for example, noted for its forgettable tag lines. These epithets, some for companies now merged into others, inspire no one, sound alike, are often silly, change frequently, and as Macbeth would say, signify nothing.

- "The right relationship is everything" —JP MORGAN CHASE
  Am I using a dating service?

- "Follow your lead" —NATIONAL CITY
  Who's my master and where's the leash?

- "Whatever it takes" —BANK ONE
  Uh, so illegal activity is okay?

- "Ideas for the way you live" —BARNETT BANK
  Do banks really do decorating?

- "You're not just invested, you're personally invested"
  —FIDELITY
  Gee, and all along I thought it was someone else's money!

- "Make life rewarding" —AMERICAN EXPRESS
  Uh huh, and all I have to do is buy stuff?

- "Forward thinking" —FLEET
  Better than backward, I suppose.

Successful tag lines are distinctive and reflect the focal point of the company. They should capture the image of the company's brand head-on. With a pinpoint tag line, the consumer should be able to instantly identify an industry, or even better, a company. Solid tag lines should stand the test of time and rarely, if ever, change. Ideally, it should describe or be your company's unique selling proposition. Be specific. Be relevant. Be exciting.

Here are some examples of time-tested slogans that immediately conjure up their companies' names. The Nike slogan is the youngest; it has been around about fifteen years. Many of the others have been in use for twenty-five years or longer and are recognizable to millions of people, instantly.

- "This Bud's for you"
- "Just do it"
- "You're in good hands with Allstate"
- "Frosted Flakes...they're grrrrreat!"
- "When you care enough to send the very best"
- "It takes a licking and keeps on ticking"
- "The Citi never sleeps"
- "Get Met, it pays"
- "When it absolutely, positively has to get there overnight"
- "When EF Hutton talks, people listen"
- "We are looking for just a few good men"

Another important ingredient in the creation of a powerful and meaningful tag line is the use of mnemonics and jingles. Few companies use either one today, and the ability of consumers to remember their slogans is dramatically reduced.

Take General Electric's long-time slogan: "GE, we bring good things to life." It's actually difficult to write without singing it out loud. GE went against the grain, took an ordinary line that any company could claim, and made it their worldwide slogan. By putting their name in the tag line and using it across all their businesses, they created an uplifting jingle that gained worldwide recognition for forty years.

Just a few months into 2003, GE changed their slogan to "Imagination at work." It remains to be seen how successful this slogan will be.

The decision to change a tag line merits serious consideration. For some reason, it became fashionable to change tag lines in the '90s. Many companies did so on a regular basis, and a few even made changes within the span of one year.

This constant upheaval makes the whole exercise worth-less. No one, not your employees, your customers, your potential customers, can be expected to keep up with various versions of what your business stands for. It reminds me of a story about Rosser Reeves, a legend at the Ted Bates Agency in the '40s and the '50s, and a brilliant creative with a prickly personality—not a surprise among creative types!

As the story goes, a client confronted him one day and asked why he should continue to pay a substantial annual fee when the same ad ran time after time, year after year, without ever changing. Reeves replied, "To keep your people from changing what I've done."

Truer words were never spoken. Companies and agencies should agree to a tag line that everyone can get behind, one that is shorthand for what that company is really all about, and then stick with the line forever.

Should Companies with Many Divisions Use One Slogan, Worldwide?

The answer is yes. Especially at large companies, management needs to telegraph to employees, customers, and Wall Street that theirs is a company with a primary focus that all parties recognize. And it is most important with global employees who need to remember they really are part of one entity, no matter what country they work in or what product they offer.

Here are a few guidelines to help you create a great tag line:

1 Think about incorporating your company name into the tag line.

2 Try to use a phrase that really rings true with all employees, no matter what division or job skill. Example: "In God we trust," all Americans.

3 Even if you don't operate worldwide, assume you do.

4 Don't throw out an old tag line because it's old. In fact, you might have an old line that could be brought back or updated.

5 Don't create a tag line by committee.

6 Secure management commitment for a ten-year minimum usage of any new line.

7 If you utilize TV or company video presentations, by all means use motion or a jingle to bring your tag line to life. An effective technique is to show three lines that flash in sequence on the screen and then dissolve into your company logo. Why three? Because three lines can build visual excitement, keep the viewer focused for the last ten seconds of the ad or presentation, and leave an upbeat, positive, lasting impression.

Think Globally, Act Locally ... to a Point

ALL TRULY SUCCESSFUL marketing programs have one element in common: they can be duplicated anywhere in the world. Your company, your product, your service, should have the same positioning, same visual elements, and the same basic personality, everywhere.

Sure, local language needs to be carefully crafted, but don't listen to half-baked arguments like, "oh, that will never work in this market" or "people are really different over here." Ninety-nine percent of the time it will work, and in today's truly global economy, if every country has a completely different campaign, you will confuse consumers, lose business, and waste money.

Acting globally does not mean you have to use the same spokesperson in all markets. Quite the contrary, using local or

Q & A Format

Regardless of their culture, people are compelled to look at a question and want to know the answer. This format in any written material is guaranteed to increase readership. Consider the use of the Q & A format 90 percent of the time in your promotional materials. You will definitely notice a difference in response to what you print.

regional personalities is fine and makes sense given the vast difference in people and customs worldwide. But layouts can remain the same, positioning can remain the same, and the overall sales message should be very similar from market to market.

There are lots of examples of companies that practice global marketing effectively—McDonald's, Coke, IBM, HSBC, Nike, most international airlines, the mobile phone industry, and even individual country tourism campaigns. Countries like Bermuda, Mexico, and Canada have been promoting themselves for years in a consistent fashion, worldwide.

I remember when the Concorde first went into service in the '70s. British Airways came out with a universally understood campaign headlined by two words that needed no translation anywhere: TIME MACHINE.

Is every product or service capable of global reach and recognition by consumers? Of course not. McDonald's does not serve beef hamburgers in India and it does serve wine in France to "kids" of all ages. Your core product can be marketed consistently around the world most of the time. McDonald's is in the fast food business everywhere. It provides quick and easy dining everywhere. It promotes great value for the buck or yen or rial, everywhere. These features can be depicted globally in consistent, integrated advertising.

On the other hand, the menu at McDonald's will change from market to market, based on local eating customs. Clearly, companies that operate in multiple countries need to recognize the local market conditions and create products for a single market when demand is strong enough to warrant the investment.

The main point to remember is that most of the time, you should be able to present your core business in a consistent and compelling manner, everywhere.

Integration Wins Wars and the Mind of the Consumer

THE WAR IN IRAQ, in 2003, was the first time American fighting forces—Army, Navy, Air Force, Marines, and Special Ops—were truly integrated into one seamless command structure and offensive powerhouse. Previous to this foray, the last major leap in military integration was the German blitz movement of planes and tanks in the opening months of World War II. Both military operations were enormously successful.

There is an important lesson here for marketers: all media must work together simultaneously in order to have a significant effect on the outcome of a campaign. It is way better to mount a two-month course of action that includes television, print, radio, outdoor, Web, direct mail—all with a common call to action—than to commit to a year of just television spots.

An excellent case study is the MCI story—not the scandals of the past few years, but rather the success of an incredible early growth strategy. Beginning in the '80s, MCI transformed itself from a small, struggling, long-distance alternative to Ma Bell to THE other major player in the long-distance market. Over a two-year period, they employed a blitzkrieg approach to marketing their residential and commercial services in a totally integrated fashion.

On a systematic basis, MCI went from major city market to major city market with an intense six-week multimedia blitz. This was marketing integration in a highly effective yet rarely done form, mainly because it takes so much coordination and pre-planning. MCI also went back into each market for a "cleanup" campaign six months after the initial blitz.

The war analogy is not accidental. MCI really thought of itself as waging war against AT&T. Put in a military context, they were a highly organized guerilla warfare unit at war with the army of occupation, AT&T.

Since they could not even remotely match AT&T's national ad budget, MCI basically fed off each market success, a strategy that allowed them to spend far less than AT&T. For a few million dollars in multimedia expenditures, MCI entered a market for six weeks, built up a new customer base with new cash flow, and then leveraged the new liquidity to enter the next market.

Doing some simple math, if you spend $6 million in one market for six weeks, you have an impact of almost $52 million annualized. With this kind of penetration, consumers will remember ads for many months after they have run—especially if the creative and product offer are strong and memorable. In MCI's case their offer was simple and effective: for the same phone time, you will save a bundle using MCI versus AT&T.

MCI presented this comparison very effectively by showing two side-by-side gas pump meters, one labeled MCI, and the other AT&T. The camera rolled with the two pumps "filling up phone time" for different length calls, graphically making the point that MCI could clearly save you from 20 to 60 percent based on the call length and route. This visual comparison was used in all forms of advertising, in all markets to make the same simple point over and over again: "MCI saves you money on every call you make. Ma Bell is ripping you off. It's easy to switch. Be a smart consumer and show Ma Bell who's boss."

To continue the earlier military analogy, your "troops" have to be highly trained and motivated. And they have to believe in your product. MCI's management made their troops believers. All employees used the service and saw the savings, firsthand. All of them were given stock options and stock bonuses at a time when most companies just handed out stock to the big guys. All employees could articulate their mission—to replace Ma Bell—an out-of-touch behemoth that was ripping off the American family and attempting to prevent normal competition in the marketplace. The MCI troops were a lean, mean, fighting-for-a-noble-cause machine. And they positively infected MCI's new customers with the same "we're in this together" mentality.

MCI's early years were integration in its purest and most powerful form. Their blitzkrieg strategy extended to nonstop attacks on Capitol Hill and the FCC, activities that generated constant publicity and raised awareness of the need for reform in the long-distance phone market. MCI even moved its headquarters from Chicago to Washington, D.C., to be closer to the legislative action and to show their commitment to facing the enemy head-on. MCI encouraged their customers to join them in this fight and on their monthly

The Enemy

If your business doesn't have a major competitor, then make one up. Every company needs an enemy, a competitor to fight against, to rally the troops around and provide additional meaning to their jobs. It gives purpose to your efforts to have some entity to try to put out of business. Think of the Cold War and we the Capitalists versus those misguided Communists. Think of the whole concept of sports. In political campaigns, an attack on the "enemy," the other candidate, is a major part of the job.

Business is a contest with winners and losers. You do not just serve customers, you act preemptively to steal them from competitors before competitors do the same to you.

bills brilliantly reminded them of their savings versus AT&T on each call.

I worked with the management of MCI in those incredible growth years and have never seen a more dedicated, coordinated, integrated marketing effort emanating from every single employee every day. Truly remarkable.

During this same period, an unlikely group gained fame and fortune with some of the best use of integrated marketing I have ever seen. In the '80s, the TV evangelists came into their own, harnessed the power of integrated marketing, and made a spectacular increase in the size of their ministries. My agency colleagues and I worked firsthand with almost every major evangelist in the nation: Oral Roberts, Jerry Falwell,

Rex Humbart, Jim Baker, Pat Robertson, and others. It was an amazing lesson learned.

All of these men were star performers who had been on the preaching circuit since an early age. Although I am not a big fan of zealots, religious or otherwise, working with these fellows and their staffs made me a believer in their genuine commitment to doing good deeds in the fields of health and education, and their devotion to the followers who provided the funds to make it all happen.

These preachers shared another very important trait: they totally understood integrated marketing, inside and out. For starters, like the memorable personalities described in Chapter Four, they knew how to make themselves compelling spokesmen. They also knew how to entertain their audiences and consistently focused on their unique selling proposition: "We are all children of God put on this earth as sinners and yet able to achieve eternal life if we ask His forgiveness and seek His blessings." Hard to argue with a unique selling proposition that promises a pass into heaven for going along with the program!

Similar to the MCI situation, there was a large untapped audience in America looking for a good deal. In this case, the core audience was about 3 to 5 million 65-and-older women and men who could not, or did not, participate in their local church activities. For some it was health problems that kept them housebound. For others it was just too far to drive to the nearest fundamentalist church. Often, the local preachers were boring and uninspiring. Add to this core audience another 20 to 30 million born-again Christians, and therein lies a market waiting to be excited by a better offer, one far more compelling than traditional church "marketing."

Through the miracle of television, the top preachers were incredibly successful and collectively raised billions of dollars for their schools, hospitals, churches, overseas missions, and various pet projects. This accomplishment was based on three actions established churches could not perform.

1 They used the power of television to come directly into every home and provided real entertainment in the name of God—great singing, great acting, great fund raising.

2 They stayed on message through a coordinated, round-the-clock media effort. Oral Roberts for instance had a twice weekly television show, a daily radio show, frequent television specials, books, records, weekly newsletters, all with the same message: "Tell me your troubles, your sins, your ailments, your concerns for you and your family and friends, and I will personally pray for you and them over and over again. And of course, to keep my ministry going so I can keep praying for sinners and save souls, send me whatever you can spare as often as you can."

They spent millions to build, refine, and invent new and creative ways to harness the computer to maintain detailed records of the millions who responded to their on-air 800 numbers and direct mail. They hired the best database experts on the planet, my company at the time, to give them complete state-of-the-art computer letter capability. In a matter of days after a "customer" called or wrote in, a letter would be sent highlighting the details of their individual situation and offering what actually amounted to a one-on-one prayer session.

3 So-called organized religion never knew what hit it and still, to this day, is unable to marshal the resources to serve those who wish to call and write, and to receive personal attention in return.

Clearly, for marketing to run on all cylinders and blow away the competition, all media have to work together, all the time. Be careful not to send confusing or contradictory messages. Colleges do this all the time. They mail glossy alumni bulletins showing the campus in all its brilliance and at the same time send fund-raising letters that stress their dire financial condition. What message are you supposed to believe?

Be sure ongoing public relations, internal employee communications, and customer communications are added to the mix. And remember, the media "song book" has to be the same for every point of contact with employees and customers to truly make an impact.

Location, Location, Location: Get the Most from Your Media Dollars

MEDIA PLANNERS throw around lots of acronyms, like CPM (cost per thousand) and GRP (gross rating points), that relate to the cost of reaching people through various media: print, TV, radio, Internet. But these terms, and a bunch more, have no bearing on whether the target audience actually sees your ad, enjoys it, and does something in response.

A colleague of mine from Citigroup likes to remind her marketing team that media planning is 60 percent art and 40 percent science. I might even bump the art percentage up to 70.

There are a lot of factors, some in your control and many not, that influence whether an ad campaign gets noticed by the right individuals and contributes to the success of the product or service that is advertised.

Three of the most critical factors are ones that you actually can control:

Visual impact: The ad or series of ads should be visually compelling and demand attention from the viewer or reader.

Location: You pay for the very best "real estate." You'll need that space in the publication or spot on TV or radio that will most likely be seen or heard by the maximum number of people who fit your target profile.

Frequency: Within your budget, you should strive to maximize the number of times an ad appears.

Despite all the graphs and charts and mind-numbing numbers that media experts throw at you, these are the three factors that really count.

Much of this book is devoted to the number one factor, the creation of a compelling ad. The rest of this chapter will focus on the simple rules I follow to maximize media dollars through optimal placement and ad frequency.

There is no doubt that media planners at ad agencies around the world are a dedicated bunch who really thrive on their specialized craft. But they have a tendency to spread your media budget among as many media outlets as possible —broad reach, as they call it. You have another goal, which is much more critical to getting noticed. As I mention above, it's called frequency.

Are you better off having an ad appear a few times over a year in thirty magazines and newspapers, or very frequently in ten? The effect of frequency trumps occasional placements every time, even if you appear more frequently in fewer publications.

Hand in hand with frequency is prime location. The only way to insure most readers see your ad is to pay for premium positioning in every publication you buy space in.

None of us have unlimited budgets. In fact, usually we have fewer dollars to work with than we want. The best use of these dollars is to narrow down the publications and pay the extra dollars required to buy premium space. The space that every reader is most likely to see. Where might that be? Here are some tips.

Print Media

Magazines: Top spots for readership are back cover, inside front cover, inside back cover, across from the table of contents (if it is easily found), and opposite popular sections in the publication.

Newspapers: Number one spot is page three, first section. Back page, first section is right up there. After that, it depends on the layout of the newspaper, what section makes sense for your product or service, and what section offers fewer ads from the competition.

In order to secure these top spots, you have to pay over and above normal rates. Prime real estate is all about location: a house on the beach costs more than a larger house a block inland. Same with media. Why pay any amount of money for a space somewhere in the publication that the vast majority of readers will either skim over or never see? Let the other guys do that.

Woody Allen once said, "Eighty percent of life is just showing up." Ad placement is a little trickier. It must be where most readers go instinctively, where they are likely to go every time they pick up the publication in question.

Most media planning is not mysterious. You need to decide who your target audience is, what their media habits are likely

93

to be, and determine the most visible locations in the publication. Then buy those spots as often as possible.

Here's what the Bose Corporation, a maker of high-quality, moderately priced sound equipment, does to maintain visibility with the right audience week after week. Without fail, Bose takes out a full-page black and white ad every single week in the *New York Times Magazine*. For years, they have placed a product ad in about the same spot, close to the back cover and often across from the Sunday crossword puzzle. Who does it appeal to? Well, to anybody who likes high-quality sound gear at a reasonable price. These same people tend to be thoughtful, well-educated, and undaunted by an ad that goes into a bit of technical detail. Many of them also like to work the Sunday crossword puzzle, or spend an hour or more by themselves, in peaceful, quiet solitude. Listening to music is often enjoyed in a similar environment. In fact, music is a perfect backdrop for puzzle fanatics. There is a new puzzle every week. There is a Bose ad every week. Makes sense.

Bose's unorthodox placement in the *New York Times Magazine* is a great example of another element of successful media placement: go where all your competitors don't. Sure there are magazines targeted to audio enthusiasts and they are jam-packed with sound equipment ads. What are your chances of really getting noticed in those publications, especially when surrounded by competitors' ads? Stand out from the pack. Think outside the box. Go wild.

Women's fashion advertising is a case in point. Pick up any issue of *Vanity Fair* magazine, that is, if you are strong enough to lift it. There are so many fashion ads, page after page after page, that the feature articles seem almost like afterthoughts. Will any one ad get noticed? It all goes back to the art of media placement.

All financial services companies want to advertise in the same business sections of newspapers, and their ads are usually densely clustered in those pages. But what about the sections less populated by competitors, like the sports section, or automotive, or even the real estate section? There's a high probability your ad will stand out in those pages.

The go-where-no-one-else-goes strategy is worth serious consideration. It seems to work for Bose or they wouldn't be in the *New York Times Magazine* Sunday after Sunday, week after week, year after year.

TV and Radio Placement

The same rules in print media apply to these two options: excite the viewer or listener with your message, be in the most visible spot possible, be there as much as possible.

Ads are annoying on TV. They do allow bathroom breaks, but still, no one likes these constant interruptions. The one big exception to this rule is the Super Bowl, when the ads have become a game unto themselves and often spark more discussion the day after than the football outcome.

But whether you place an ad on a 2 a.m. late show or plunk down $2 million for a Super Bowl spot, the most desirable position is the first ad spot in the first commercial break. You are far better off having one ad every week for a year in the first commercial break of a weekly show than multiple ads for a few months in the same show.

Like a magazine's inside front cover, this position is where the largest number of viewers is likely to notice the ad. Again, just like in a magazine where readership drops off the further into the magazine you go, ad viewership drops off 95 percent of the time after the first commercial break. Depending on the show, it may not drop significantly, but it is still extremely rare for ad viewership to increase as a show progresses.

Now, thanks to the wonders of technology, the biggest threat to TV advertising is TiVo® and every other form of digital video recorder (DVR). A study of consumer TV habits completed by Forrester Research in 2004 points out that when people watch pre-recorded shows they skip 92 percent of the commercials. Not good news for advertisers or the TV industry.

And DVR usage is on the upswing. In 2004, there were at least 5 million households with ad-skipping capability, and by 2009 half of all American households will have this capability. Where does this leave viewership of the TV spot you spend all that time and money to produce?

The best defense against ad skipping will continue to be advertising on shows that are least likely to be recorded for later viewing. The two categories that lead the pack are news and sports. The same 2004 Forrester study notes that 93 percent of viewers with delayed viewing options continue to watch local news in real time. Following local news in real time popularity is national news, sports events, and special events like the Oscars or Emmys.

Clearly, news and sports shows will become more desirable to TV advertisers in the years ahead. In addition, television producers will try to combat ad skipping with the creation of more real time, interactive events for viewers to participate in during scheduled programming. Whether viewers want to be active as well as passive remains to be seen.

Radio is a great medium. You can buy local markets very easily and the cost to produce radio spots is peanuts compared to TV. There is no TiVo® to worry about—radio is 100 percent real time, and ad placement is pretty simple: Drive Time,

Drive Time, Drive Time. Prime time radio is 6:00 to 8:30 a.m. and 4:30 to 7:30 p.m.

Radio is overlooked by a lot by marketers and it shouldn't be. Radio is a terrific low-cost way to get your message out daily in a specific market. It's also an effective vehicle for advertising in fringe markets without a huge investment.

Radio is great for small businesses and not-for-profit organizations that want to reach a broad audience and just cannot afford TV.

Commuting by car is here to stay and there are more cars on the road every year. You should take advantage of this fact and seriously consider radio as part of most marketing campaigns.

Global Media Planning and Placement

The good news is that global media planning gets easier all the time. Up until just a few years ago, it was almost impossible to get the giant media companies to provide a single point of contact with knowledge of region by region media options. With the steady progression of the global economy, media companies have woken up and most now provide staff who can handle the placement of advertising in any region of the world.

As you might expect, there are specific regional challenges to media buying outside of the United States. Latin America is an extremely difficult region to plan advertising. TV viewership is hard to pin down and there are few magazines that have any significant circulation, especially business publications. What's more, direct mail is unreliable and costly. Africa is even more difficult. Fortunately, the major developed-world countries are fairly straightforward and are not all that different from the United States.

97

In terms of creative, there are country-specific issues, but most are manageable. As a rule, a global marketing campaign should have the same look and feel in every country where the product or service is being offered. The basic sales message is often pretty much the same, although local language will dictate different slants to make the same point.

Often you run across tactical issues such as whether to include English in part of an ad that is in a different local language. In Japan, for instance, headlines and punch lines are often in English. English is viewed as hip and cool when used in these two ways.

In some Arabic-speaking countries, the locals like their ads in Arabic but prefer the call to action in English or in both languages.

When you go global, an agency's worth really gets tested. Insist on working with an ad agency with solid global experience. Fortunately, most agencies today are part of a global network with experts in each region of the world. Your core team should be able to tap into that local expertise and present you with a coherent and comprehensive plan for whatever product you want to promote in multiple countries.

No One Ever Bought Anything from an English Professor

So, DO NOT WRITE LIKE ONE.

Think of the opening of a promotional letter as a headline that needs to grab reluctant readers and draw them in—like the one-line paragraph that opens this chapter. To guarantee readership, a letter, unless it's from the IRS, needs short sentences, very short paragraphs, some just one sentence long, and a ton of white space, which is pleasing to the eye, much like a well-crafted brochure.

Salutations get in the way. I suggest you leave them out. "Dear Friend" is just plain annoying—I am not your friend and I don't know you. Dear Reader…Dear Colleague…Dear Employee. They all telegraph one message you should avoid: this is a form letter going to hundreds, thousands, or millions of people. Why remind your audience that they are one of so many? Immediately open with a headline and you are way ahead of all the other "Dear Friend" letters out there.

Those of us who write promotional letters for a living are routinely asked how long a letter should be for maximum impact. My answer is worthy of any politician's mushy response to a direct question: the letter should be as long as is necessary to tell the story. Given current attention levels, my general advice is to stick to one-page letters most of the time. If a product has a lot of features and options, you can provide an attachment with the details and thus keep the actual letter as short as possible.

My favorite example of "short can be way better than long" comes from the world of fund raising, an industry where letter writing has been a core competency for decades. One of the most successful fund-raising letters ever written was three short sentences written by a television evangelist facing a bigger than usual financial crisis in his ministry. He sent 2 million one-page letters to his database of previous contributors. Each letter simply read: "Major financial crisis. No time to explain now. Please send anything you can!"

…And they did.

Back to that short attention span, which can often work in your favor. No one remembers the content of a letter. Sure, you remember you received a letter asking for money, or selling a subscription, but you rarely remember the actual wording. If you craft a promotional letter that really works, you can use it with very little modification over and over and over again.

Years ago, John Groman, a world-class direct marketing dynamo, wrote a fund-raising letter for the Boston Symphony. The letter was so effective that the symphony used the exact same letter for five years in a row to kick off their annual fund-raising campaign. The only thing that changed was the date. Each year the letter was mailed to about 50,000 followers of the symphony. The symphony never received a single phone call or letter asking why they sent the exact same letter each year. Instead, all they received were record-level donations.

In the commercial world, the *Wall Street Journal* has used the same subscription prospecting letter for close to twenty-five years. Sure, professional letter writers notice—all three of us—but no one else does, or cares.

If you happen on a promotional letter that gets great response from your customers and/or prospects, let them get excited all over again next year and the year after that.

Another technique is what I call the One-Two Punch. Send a very short letter to your target audience telling them that they will receive a special mailing with an exciting offer, just for them, in a couple of days. Of course, the follow up mailing must come across as a unique or valuable offer. I have seen this One-Two strategy work for any kind of business or not-for-profit group many times. The more loyal the customer group is to your product or service, the better this technique will work.

A variation of this technique is to send a letter notifying the recipients that their response is required right away, or you will follow up this letter with a phone call. If done properly in the right tone you can dramatically boost response by "threatening" to call them.

Think More Like Armani and Less Like The Gap

English professors, not known for their sense of style, also seem to spend as little money as possible on their wardrobe. In a similar fashion, most companies stint on the cost of their mailings.

Yes/No

Humans hate to say the word "no." In some cultures, most notably Asian, people go to great lengths to avoid saying no to anyone at any time, even though that's the message they would like to deliver.

You can take advantage of this hardwiring of our universal gene pool if you always structure a customer offer with a yes/no option. Not-for-profit organizations were the first groups to use this technique widely. Lately, it seems to have disappeared from most offers, and that is a mistake.

Here is a hypothetical example of a yes/no option for The Fresh Air Fund, one of my favorite charities.

Check one and return this reply card:

___Yes, I want to contribute $____ to help send inner-city kids to summer camp to give them an experience that will last a lifetime.

___No, I don't want kids to have the experience of a few weeks of summer in the country away from the baked sidewalks and streets of New York.

I think you get the point.

Over the course of an entire decade, the following two competitors, with opposite attitudes toward marketing expenditures, raised money from their respective constituencies. No surprise, their results were radically different. The two competitors were the Democratic Senatorial Committee and the Republican Senatorial Committee, the decade, 1980 to 1990.

Given common stereotypes, you might think the Democrats raise money from millions of donors of modest means who give individual small donations. The Republicans are thought to raise large amounts from relatively few "fat cats." In fact, historically and to this day, it is just the reverse. The Democrats are much more successful with large donors and the Republicans get much more juice from millions of small donations.

The primary reason for this outcome is the care and attention each pays to the direct mail process, as evidenced by the fund-raising efforts of the two senatorial committees during the '80s. Year after year, the Republican Senatorial Committee raised more money per month than their crosstown Democrat rivals did in a full year.

Why the huge discrepancy? Surprisingly, it had little to do with the candidates' philosophies, issues of the day, wealthy donors, not-so-wealthy donors, the donkey versus the elephant, or the intelligence of their respective K Street consultants.

The point of difference was the Democrats' belief that direct mail fund-raising was all about how cheaply they could generate a letter to each of their millions of potential contributors. The Republicans, on the other hand, believed that the more you spent per piece, the more money you could raise. Ninety-five percent of the time, the Republicans were right on the money.

Republicans really went overboard in using state-of-the-art personalization in their letters, rich cotton fiber paper, embossed gold seals, and closed face envelopes. The Democrats favored a less expensive look, right down to the window envelope. Think about it—have you ever received a personal letter in a window envelope? What do you receive in window envelopes? Bills. Just bills.

The Republicans made their audience feel special, like insiders. They offered distinctive gifts for those agreeing to monthly pledges: trips to Washington to meet and greet the star politicians from the Party and special 800-number hotlines to call in their thoughts on issues.

They engaged their base with the most personal letters and offers money could buy. And they got a HUGE response. I remember a mailing (also mentioned in Chapter One) in the early '80s sent by the Republican Senatorial Committee to 200,000 previous donors asking for a special year-end donation. The letter was sent express mail and cost more than $7 per letter. This extravagant spending was absolutely unheard of in an environment where the Democrats tried to keep costs to 25 cents per letter. The result: that one letter generated more net dollars than the Democrats raised that entire year.

No matter what your political affiliation, the more you make your customers feel special via direct mail, the more receptive they will be.

12

The Three Most Important
Customer Lessons
You Will Ever Learn

Lesson One: People renew the way they are acquired.

This happens about 98 percent of the time. So for sure you might want to pay attention to this most human of human behaviors.

If you liked that first Big Mac, chances are you will have another and another and another, assuming they are consistent in look, taste, and yes, even feel. The fast food industry is a prime example of this customer axiom. Customers return because they have the same eating experience every single time.

On the other hand, the auto industry has not always paid attention to this rule. Many car manufacturers have had new car dreams dashed by altering the original design that brought the customer in the door in the first place. Remember the original Ford Thunderbird? It was a beautiful, new, sexy addition to the Ford lineup and generated many new customers addicted to its sporty look. After almost forty years of grim style changes and poor sales, Ford realized its design tinkering was a disaster, and too late, tried to go back to where it began. Chevy Corvette fared better right from the beginning, by sticking close to the original Sting Ray design and keeping its high horsepower intact.

Even ice cream conforms to this customer renewal law. Ben & Jerry's started out as a "chunky" super premium brand. A few years ago they expanded to smooth flavors, with almost no success. Subsequently, they backed away from that part of the super premium category and have retained a strong customer base.

Clothing, drugs, dog food, toilet paper, nothing is immune to the law of customer renewal. There is even some evidence that many people who marry for a second or third time continue to marry people with the same characteristics as their previous partners. Italy has the lowest birth rate in the world and has for some time. Why? Italian men are so pampered by their mothers that they just settle into mom's home and care, and literally never leave—talk about renewing the way you are acquired!

Customer promotions are not immune to this rule, either. If you acquire a customer through a special price offer, do not expect him to renew without a similar offer. PBS learned this the hard way. Years ago, all PBS stations across the country began to offer merchandise as a come-on for voluntary contributions. Thirty years later, the vast majority of their donors are first and foremost merchandise loyal: no merchandise—

umbrellas, coffee mugs, CDs, beach blankets, and so forth—no donation. Now these PBS stations are hooked and must continue the giveaway. If you get on this type of merchandise treadmill, just remember it is almost impossible to get off.

No matter what you sell, the successful renewal offer is one that is similar, or better than, the offer the customer responded to originally.

Lesson Two: The most critical time in a new customer's relationship with your business is the first week after her initial purchase.

Psychologically, all new customers require some kind of reinforcement: they need to know they did the right thing by purchasing your product or service. It is your job to alleviate that post-purchase anxiety and make customers feel good about their transaction. Right away.

With e-business, it is very easy to send an e-mail thanking each customer for his purchase as soon as you receive a record of it. Think confirmation and thank you wrapped up in one e-mail response. Many companies do just that today, from Amazon to Fandango to *The New Yorker's* Cartoon Bank. But if your business is not Web-based, don't let that stop you. You should make sure you capture every new customer's e-mail on file as part of a sign-up procedure.

What about a real letter or postcard instead of an e-mail? This is perfectly okay. For years, many upscale retailers have sent personalized communications thanking customers for their most recent purchase. Just remember, a letter or postcard only works when you send it immediately after the transaction. If it takes weeks for the customer to receive your communication, it can look like you have some huge, impersonal system that cranks these things out automatically. Better to send nothing than to remind them they are basically just a computer record somewhere in Idaho. Written thank-you notes only work when they are received within five business days of the purchase. Well, maybe even six or seven days, but no more than that.

The following story will help you understand the critical nature of a quick reply after a customer has experienced a major negative transaction.

Back in the late '80s, my wife, Faye, worked on the Dell Computer account for Chiat/Day, an advertising agency in New York City. Dell is headquartered in Austin, Texas, which necessitated her flying between there and New York on a regular basis. American was the only major airline that made the trip, with a stop in Dallas. Most of her flights went smoothly but on one occasion, the first leg from New York to Dallas was severely delayed because of fog in Dallas. The plane circled and circled and finally landed in Dallas two hours behind schedule and too late for Faye to make the connection to Austin in time for her meeting. She had to turn around and come back to New York. Well, these things happen, bad weather disrupts air schedules.

About five weeks later, Faye received a personalized letter from American Airlines. The letter began with an apology for the delay of her flight five weeks ago. It went on to say that despite this weather-caused delay, American strived to get customers to their destinations on time. As a small token of appreciation for her frequent flyer status, they automatically credited her frequent flyer account with an additional 2,500 miles.

Faye showed me the letter and I was impressed. American had all the data right. They took the time to apologize and provide some solace with extra miles that Faye never expected. It appeared to be a real class act. I said to Faye, "Gee, these guys have really done a good job to make amends for that nightmare flight you had last month." She didn't agree. "They are four weeks too late," she said.

And she was right.

Ironically, the best time to ask customers for additional business is right after they buy something from you or pay off a long-standing obligation. Think what might happen if a bank thanked a customer who has just paid off a loan, and mentioned, in the same letter, that they would gladly give him another one right away. Omaha Steaks, a mail order food company, understands this concept in spades. When you call, the phone representatives are likely to mention that everything in the catalog is actually cheaper than listed because you are a repeat customer. If you are a first-time customer, they will offer a similar discount. This is an example of attacking post-purchase anxiety before the purchase. Smart? You bet, and way better than Prozac.

Lesson Three: Forget complicated clusters and demographics.

There are all kinds of books and studies and doctoral dissertations on long-winded matrix descriptions of customer groups. Most of it is so complicated that you will never be able to create a marketing program to fit the endless customer clusters, as some experts call them, or even to identify these clusters within your customer universe in the first place.

In my experience there are five basic customer groups. These groupings are easy to understand and have behavior patterns that will respond to a well-designed marketing strategy.

1 The Evangelists: they love you, period. They cannot say enough good things about your company or product. And if you keep asking for the order, they will keep on buying. Devotees like these deserve all kinds of positive reinforcement, from exclusive "insider" communications to an onslaught of special offers. Special does not necessarily mean cheaper pricing by the way, special means...well, special. Something your other customers do not have access to. After all, this group usually represents 90 percent of your profit.

2 On the Fence: they buy occasionally. They are often somewhat price sensitive or feel like you do not always have the best product for their needs. They require compelling reasons to increase their business with you—an exciting offer, special customer service, a positive comparison of your product to the competition's, or just something new and different. This is clearly an important customer group and is often the largest in size. Out of this group come the Evangelists of tomorrow. If you manage to do a good job with only these first two customer groupings, your business will likely thrive and grow year after year.

3 The Price Is Right: they probably bought from you once, responding to a solid price offer. Most of these customers will never change and will only shop price. If you have the lowest price point on the planet in your category, by all means tell them, just like Wal-Mart does again and again. When marketing to this group, remember price motivates them and probably nothing else ever will.

4 Negative: they had a bad experience in the purchasing cycle, perhaps a frustrating customer service interaction. A telltale sign of this customer group is they bought once and that was that. So just forget about them, right? Well, not necessarily. I know several organizations that are quite successful in converting some of these customers to On the Fence and even to Evangelists. Their technique is to send a very lengthy apology letter that addresses the customer's bad experience head-on and admits that the company is not always perfect: "Yes, we fail sometimes. We hate it when we do, but it happens. We are human after all. Please let us make amends and be given a second chance." Note: If you receive a complaint letter, phone call, or e-mail, it is very important that your apology letter go out immediately after the complaint is received, preferably the same day.

5 No Clue. Yes, there are these people on every customer list. They often do not even know they are a customer. Perhaps they bought once by mistake or were given your product as a gift. Just make sure that you treat them like any other prospect. They are not really a customer.

Don't Go Cold Turkey with Your Best Customers

Now that you understand who your customers are, it is time to focus on how to treat them. When someone identifies himself as a very good customer, the natural reaction of most companies, large and small, is to stop communicating with him. They erroneously believe they run the risk of irritating a great customer by sending him too many letters or e-mails with more offers. Of course, when you cease communication or reduce it from previous levels, your message to the customer is, "You aren't important to us anymore."

Do not fall into this trap. Remember, your competitors are still trying to get the attention of your best customers any chance they can. Most well-run not-for-profit organizations understand the importance of continual but appropriate communication with their best contributors. Their organization's health and well-being is based on constantly presenting their case directly to the people who can really make a difference, financially.

In business, marketers always focus on the 20/80 rule: 80 percent of a company's revenue comes from 20 percent of its customers. Fair enough. But not-for-profits went one step further and have determined that 50 percent of their revenue comes from just 1 percent of their contributors.

If companies do the research and really pick apart the 20 percent representing their best customers, they will generally find a 10/90 rule, which says a mere 10 percent of customers generate 90 percent of the revenue. That 10 percent is a group that most definitely needs special care, attention, and an ongoing dialogue. It is manageable enough in size for a team of your best marketing people to focus on.

Sometimes this dialogue takes the form of special service that companies like Fidelity, Schwab, American Express, Hertz, and retailers like Saks and Tiffany provide for their very best customers. For example, it can be constant reinforcement at the cash register. Barnes & Noble has a frequent book buyers club with automatic discounts at checkout on every book or item purchased in one of their stores or online. Or, it can be a special add-on to your service, such as the way car dealers reward their best customers with hassle-free use of a courtesy car when their cars are in for service. It can even be like the communications Fidelity and Schwab send their top customers: a special quarterly magazine with content targeted at the very-high-net-worth family.

The more activity a customer has with your business, the more she should be recognized through communication, service, and/or price. Whatever the interaction, it should be relevant, topical, and frequent.

The Guthrie Lesson

In the early '80s, the highly acclaimed Guthrie Theater in Minneapolis found itself in difficult financial straits. They signed on as a client and wanted us to create their first-ever direct mail fund-raising campaign to loyal season ticket holders.

As might be expected, Guthrie's management was nervous about the solicitation and just about came unhinged a week before the scheduled drop date. They called daily with a constant battery of questions: "What if some people complain?" "What if they write nasty letters back?" "What if we get subscription cancellations?" What if, what if....

My response was a simple one, based on years of hard-won experience. Yes, I told them, you will get all of the above. I can guarantee it. You are mailing to 50,000 people. You will raise a lot of much-needed money. And yes, you will also get "hate mail." In fact, the more powerful the letter, the greater the number of disgruntled responses that will land in your mailbox.

"Is there a way to prevent this hate mail?" they asked. "Yes," I said, "the solution is to cancel the mailing and raise no money."

They went ahead with the mailing and continue their Annual Appeal to this day.

Lesson: Whenever you communicate with large numbers of people, you will hear unwanted comments from a very small percentage of the group. That's just the way it goes. Don't ever let a few complainers dictate how you conduct your overall communications program.

The Art of Building
Effective Loyalty Programs

BACK IN CHAPTER ONE where the elements that make up a winning marketing campaign are defined, I describe the success of WorldPass, Pan Am's frequent flyer program. Although they were the last major airline to launch such a program, Pan Am garnered tremendous loyalty and increased business because they totally outshined their competitors' programs. The awards were better and easier to earn. The communications were compelling. The whole look and feel of the program was very upscale. And Pan Am customers felt appreciated and special.

While every other airline paid out as little as possible to mail announcement letters and monthly statements, Pan Am spent whatever it took to look like "a million bucks" in the mail. In the initial enrollment package, a complementary round-trip coach ticket was included, good on any domestic U.S. route for six months—with no blackout dates or restrictions of any kind.

There was only one requirement. You had to enroll in the WorldPass program, fill out a reply form with your travel patterns and preferences, and pay the $25 annual program fee.

Yep, Pan Am was the first and only airline to charge frequent flyers an annual fee to enroll in its program. This action was unheard of at the time. Crazy, many pundits thought. They were dead wrong. The program flourished. Cabins filled to their highest levels in years. Participants gladly paid the fee.

Pan Am's experience illustrates the number one fundamental of a successful customer loyalty program:

The program's perceived value must exceed the perceived cost.

Over the years I have seen a lot of mushy loyalty programs where the value/cost proposition isn't clear. If customers can't figure out what the deal is, chances are they won't actively participate.

A prime example of positive perceived value centers around what American Express has accomplished with its card business. Back in 1984, American Express launched the Platinum Card, a quantum leap in charging for a piece of plastic. The annual fee was $300, and if the cardholder wanted a companion card, that was another $300. At the time, no other competitors charged more than $50 for the privilege of carrying their cards.

The Platinum Card was a winner from day one. It was elitist and only available by invitation. Very smart. It also promised way more service and card benefits, and it delivered.

American Express pointed out very clearly that the card wasn't for you unless you traveled and/or dined out extensively.

Almost fifteen years later, American Express came out with the Black Card. It has the same basic positioning as the Platinum Card, but with dramatically enhanced benefits for the frequent traveler and a service level somewhere in the stratosphere. The fee was $1,000 per card. Again, invitation only. Two years after its introduction, American Express raised the Black Card's annual fee to $2,500, but grandfathered all cardholders who were originally invited to receive the card at the initial $1,000 fee. Like with the Platinum Card, demand for the Black Card has far exceeded supply.

Can you charge more for better service? A lot more? And build customer loyalty at the same time? Clearly the answer is a big yes, IF the value is seen to outdistance the cost. The perceived value of the American Express brand adds to the proposition and enables them to create these elite cards. With high charge volume and high renewal rates, the Black and Platinum Cards are financial winners for American Express and "must haves" for every affluent world traveler.

With these two premium cards, American Express engenders very strong customer loyalty. So much so, they are the envy of the credit card industry.

The second fundamental of a solid loyalty program is to

Focus on just three or four major benefits.

Marketing types tend to come up with a long list of reasons why a customer should sign up for a program. Resist that urge completely. Instead, present a few solid, compelling reasons to become a part of your special program. Often just one good reason is enough.

Take retailers, for example. Several of the major ones have frequent shopper programs that tie your purchases to a "members only" store discount.

Barneys New York: fashion-forward upscale clothing and accessories. Annual payback in real dollars that can only be spent at Barneys.

The only requirement of Barneys's FREE STUFF frequent shopper program is that members use their distinctive, classy-looking, black Barneys charge card to accumulate purchases. All charges on the card are tabulated annually and members receive a FREE STUFF charge card at the end of the year based on the total amount of their purchases. Every charge card customer knows that the more she charges, the more accumulated dollars will appear on the next year's FREE STUFF card. There are no fine print requirements or restrictions. Every purchase counts, from full-price merchandise to items on sale.

Barneys provides a simple chart that shows how many "free" dollars you will get on your FREE STUFF card based on how much you spend. When you receive your FREE STUFF card at the beginning of the next year, you have a year to use it. And, you can use the card over and over again as long as a balance remains.

Additionally, Barneys's monthly charge card statement shows you how many FREE STUFF dollars have been accumulated to date.

This is a very easy to understand and powerful customer loyalty program with a single primary benefit.

Neiman Marcus: upscale clothing and accessories. Points redeemable for merchandise at predetermined levels.

Launched in 1984, Neiman's InCircle Rewards was the first heavily promoted frequent shopper program to reach out to customers and build shopper loyalty.

InCircle members receive points for every dollar spent on their charge cards: one dollar equals one point. Once shoppers reach the 5,000-point level in any given year, they can redeem their points for merchandise. Like the Barneys program, the meter goes back to zero every December 31st at midnight; there is no carryover in points from one year to another.

Neiman Marcus spices up their program by regularly announcing double-point days when every dollar you spend equals two points. They also provide special benefits and rewards for the wealthy loyalist who spends $100,000 per year, and for the ultra-wealthy individual who finds a way to buy $1.5 million dollars worth of what Neiman Marcus has to offer.

Barnes & Noble: books, music, and related merchandise plus upscale coffee shop. Straight discount at point of purchase.

Barnes & Noble employs a basic, instant-gratification approach to their loyalty program. Consumers pay an annual $25 fee that entitles them to a 5 percent discount off everything online and 10 percent off every item in any of their stores. Members are issued a plastic card with a membership number. Forget your card? Your home telephone number allows the salesclerk to verify your membership and issue the discount.

For smaller purchase items like books and CDs, instant gratification makes a lot of sense. You see your member benefit immediately with every item you buy, right at the time of purchase. Nothing could be easier.

Online brokers are another group that provides just a few benefits to their most loyal customers. They have adopted the age-old, straightforward approach to building loyalty and reward customers for volume of business.

Schwab, Fidelity, E*Trade, et al. use a very basic pitch: the more you trade, the cheaper the individual transaction. They position their service as being dramatically cheaper per trade than the so-called full-service brokers, and it is. If you trade only a few times per year you might be charged $25 to $30 per trade. If you trade at least monthly, that transaction charge might drop to $15. If you trade quite frequently, it will drop to below $10.

The online brokers also recognize clients who show their loyalty by keeping a lot more money in their accounts than the average client does. So even if a client with, say, a million dollars in his account initiates only an occasional trade, he will still be charged the very best rate—the same rate that applies to the frequent trader.

Although these customer loyalty strategies seem straight-forward, it is essential to think through your attitude toward loyalty rewards and make sure they are based on reality and common sense.

Fresh out of college in the '70s, I lived in The People's Republic of Cambridge. This was more than a fond nick-name—capitalism and rewarding customer loyalty were frowned on and often not allowed.

One spring day, a friend of mine ventured into his favorite Cambridge running shop to buy some shoes. A reasonably frequent customer of the store, he bought shoes there every three to four months. He wore size twelve and favored a specific type of running shoe made by a relatively obscure manufacturer. The clerk checked the stockroom and brought back a pair to try on. My friend was pleased that his shoe was in stock and thought, gee, if they had a few pairs he would just buy them all and save himself a couple of future trips to the store. He asked how many pairs were in stock.

"Three," replied the clerk.

"Great, I'll take all three," my friend said.

"No can do," said the clerk. "I just can't sell you all three pairs and have none left for other customers."

My friend said, "Do you actually sell these shoes very often?"

"Very infrequently," said the clerk, "but that's our policy—one pair per customer."

You just can't make this stuff up. Sometimes overzealousness can go awry, as it did and maybe still does, in Cambridge, Massachusetts.

Loyalty in the Not-for-Profit World

An earlier chapter in this book highlights the "golden rule" of marketing. This rule should be displayed in a prominent place on every desk of every person who engages in any form of marketing, and charities and universities are no exception.

People renew the way they are acquired.

When someone graduates from college and becomes a lifetime prospect for annual giving, what will resonate best with that person? The answer: a reminder of how her experiences during her years at that institution shaped her life—the professors she had, the campus she was at, her fellow students, the political and social events she lived through as an undergraduate or graduate student.

Indeed, those schools with the most successful fund-raising efforts almost always have a strong class agent program, where peers ask peers for that annual gift—not someone in the development office far removed from the experience shared by these classmates.

Charities are no different. People make a first-time gift because of a solicitation that strikes an emotional hot button —a homeless child saved, an endangered animal species that needs protection, a city soup kitchen that must expand, a symphony that wants to remain world class. Contributors will respond to future donation requests if they have a focus similar to the one that first got their response.

People donate for a specific reason to a specific appeal. The appeal can even be seasonal. A lot of folks make all their charitable contributions in December and at no other time. Some like to give monthly. Some don't.

Whatever the specific hot button that drove that first-time contribution—it must, absolutely must, be noted in the donor's computer file so that your institution keeps that "memory" of what triggered this first gift.

That hot button reason or season, whenever possible, should be part of the theme of every solicitation that donor receives from that point onward. There is no better way to attract additional contributions from that person.

Not-for-profits have a second very important loyalty rule:

One percent of your contributors give 50 percent of the money.

I would wager a lot of bucks that most not-for-profits spend nowhere near 50 percent of their fund-raising resources on this 1 percent. Ironically, this elite group is a very manageable size, usually 500 to 5,000 people. Yet, most organizations do not really communicate properly with them and thus leave money on the table that otherwise might be turned into a significant donation.

Here are a few simple guidelines that will help in the care and feeding of your most generous contributors.

● The top 1 percent generally gives at least 500 times more than the average donation to your organization. Whenever a donor reaches this level for the first time, the most senior official at your organization should call and thank him personally—without exception.

● All correspondence should be highly personalized. Do whatever you possibly can to make certain that top donors do not receive mass mailings and communications from your organization without an explanation. A really nice touch is to send top donors copies of mailings, newsletters, and alumni magazines that the rest of the donor base receives. Be sure to include a handwritten, FYI note "to keep you abreast of how we're communicating with donors."

● Do not be concerned about overdoing continual communications with this top group. They are invested and want to feel part of the inner circle. The more you talk to them, the happier and more committed they will feel. Believe me, they will not be irritated by the attention. They want to hear from you. Just be sure to always add the personal touch.

● They should receive a personal letter from the most senior official of your organization every other month. The communication should be centered around a "state of the ship" report as well as information about upcoming special events they might want to attend—well in advance of the actual dates.

● If you have a campus environment, invite them to come speak on their life and career. Profile these people in your newsletters and magazines. Schools rarely profile their most successful business alumni, opting instead for teachers, social workers, and other alumni with various pet social causes. This approach is fine in moderation but not to the exclusion of showcasing successful businesspeople. After all, capitalism is what keeps those Ivy doors open!

● At universities, what I call "era merchandising" can be important and is generally ignored. Not just for your top donors, but for all donors, offer mugs, jackets, hats, blankets, chairs—from their era, not the present. They will be happy to buy and you will make more money for your institution.

● Of course always ask for feedback. A special e-mail address should be set up for the best donors to send in ideas, comments, complaints, and additional contributions. Institute a system to answer any and all of their e-mails within forty-eight hours. These people are important. Make sure they feel that way.

It is a thrill to be around people who love your organization and have the means to support it at a level way above the average contributor. The more time you devote to this group the more successful your college or charity will be. An occasional phone call from your president or equivalent—at least once a year—is my final suggestion. Nothing beats individual recognition.

Surprise!
We're All Getting Older

Generation Gaps — Real and Imagined

It amazes me that so much of the marketing community, particularly TV media buyers, remains fixated on the 18 to 35 age group, when in fact the majority of disposable dollars are in the hands of adults 40 and over.

Hollywood has a similar misguided attitude toward the lion's share of moviegoers, who are ages 12 to 25. Moviemakers continue to churn out a large number of films with mature plots and serious story lines, both of which have little appeal for this age group.

Today, these two media industries seem to be able to get away with the cavalier expenditure of their marketing dollars.

But tomorrow, with its impending demographical changes, is another story.

The big news is that the global population is aging. With 22 percent of its residents 65 years or older, Florida has the highest percentage of elderly people in the United States. That statistic may come as no surprise, but you might not know Europe and Asia are right up there with Florida and in fact their populations are aging at a faster rate than in the United States and a host of Third World countries. By 2020, one-half of the population of Europe, including Russia, will be 50 or older. Japan and Singapore will also share these demographics.

An increased older population will affect every industry and every marketing plan.

The ultimate bad-case scenario for marketers is that as populations age, they tend to consume less. They drive less often. They don't care as much about the trendiest clothing. They don't need the latest computer or gadget. What's more, they downsize their housing needs and consume less food, soda, and alcohol.

Here are some more changes on the horizon:

● Some financial industry gurus fear a huge meltdown in the stock market in the next decade or two, as older investors cash out in order to pay for basic living expenses.

● The health care and drug industries will find ever-expanding markets worldwide.

● Political issues, health care, and Social Security will become more and more important in winning elections and managing the U.S. and global economies.

● Certain leisure industries will be in greater demand; golf, which is in a rut growth-wise, has bright prospects for expansion from about 2010 on.

All the above will happen in one way or another. How severely remains to be seen. The bottom line is that some industries have a bright future and some will see waning interest. This is a new demographic shift. It hasn't happened before to this degree nor in a worldwide economy, with governments and businesses interconnected in ways never imagined before.

Given the level of uncertainty associated with global aging, I've listed a few guideposts to keep in mind as you think about future marketing strategy.

- In the twenty-first century there are two basic consumer categories: adults and little adults. Maturation seems to happen at warp speed. We see young children no longer interested in dolls and dump trucks and building blocks. They want to surf the Net at age 3. They are immersed in the adult world much earlier in life than ever before. They watch more of our programs, eat the same food, and travel farther and more frequently.

- Safety, security, reliability, ease of use. These are the four big product features that consumers will base many of their buying decisions on. The products that shine in these areas will win.

- The number one nonwork activity after sleep will remain TV viewing. Even though TV seems like a dated term, the box on the wall will continue to absorb our interest, and the hours spent watching some form of programming will gradually increase. Pundits have predicted the demise of the networks for decades. They are wrong. Cable has been a huge success, but guess who owns most of the cable stations today—the networks. Actually, the biggest challenge to the entire entertainment industry is to provide enough programming to meet the demand.

● Yes, TV viewing habits will change a lot. TiVo® and other digital video recording options are here to stay and will be a huge obstacle for advertisers to surmount. In the years ahead, the majority of TV viewers will be able to watch shows at their convenience and zap the commercials in the process. This shift to viewer control will lead to a stampede to two types of programming—news and sports. Most viewers will continue to watch news updates and televised sporting events in real time. That is why broadcast of the Olympics from a distant time zone is always such a challenge. We want to see the action as it happens.

● Quality will reign supreme. It has always been the big mama of product marketing and is often the determinant for success. When you ship a package via FedEx, you expect 100 percent reliability that your package will arrive as promised. In the early years of FedEx, you expected this reliability but had no access to quality—you didn't know where your package actually was between sending point and receiving point. Today the quality of information is as important as the physical moving parts. FedEx trumped the U.S. Postal Service in package delivery because it first delivered on reliability and then used quality to put the final nail in the coffin. At one time, the U.S. Post Office controlled 98 percent of package shipments in America. Today, it's left with a mere 2 percent.

● Consumers will increasingly demand quality products that last. This is not a new trend, it just continues. In the case of the food industry this means fussier buyers of fresh food will expect top quality and will pay more for it. In the years ahead, consumers will collectively buy fewer goods, with the exception of medical products, and in many cases will pay more for superior quality.

● Personalized direct mail may make a comeback. Assuming the Post Office doesn't price itself out of business, highly personalized mail will be a tool that marketers should not ignore. Older Americans will have more time to read whatever mail they receive and may even look forward to it.

Surprisingly, there are far fewer generational gaps than ever before. Even in categories most prone to gap behavior, such as movies, music, and fashion, there is a merging of tastes not evident in past decades. Baby boomers want to look as young as possible and their kids try to look like younger versions of the parents. Music seems to be a shared activity and golden oldies are as popular as ever among all age groups. Family units still exist. Shared values remain.

The true gap that will persist in the years ahead will be between the dwindling number of younger people and the large number of older ones who depend on the younger generation to financially support their needs, in America and in many other countries around the world. We should pay close attention to the implications, opportunities, and challenges this issue will bring to bear on purchasing power and how it is used.

Marketing to the Sexes

It's all about hormones. The basic behavioral differences between men and women are influenced by these little devils throughout their entire lifetime. And it is just these differences that make a difference in successfully marketing to the sexes.

Here is a list of behaviors to consider when targeting a product or service to one sex versus another.

Impulsiveness: In general men tend to shoot from the hip and women are more reasoned in their thinking. I might wake up one day and decide to go buy a BMW. My wife isn't wired that way. A woman usually needs to think through the issues before a major expenditure on anything, even clothing. Can I afford to spend the money? Can I get a lot of use out of it? Are there good reasons to buy now as opposed to later?

From an advertising standpoint, this behavioral difference implies that women demand more information than men. Men don't need or generally want a lot of explanation, though they probably would be better off if they did. Women will actually read the fine print. Men can't be bothered. A real difference.

Practicality: You can learn a lot by observing men and women in supermarkets. There are exceptions to every rule but in general women are very sensible when they shop for food. They think value, quality, and quantity. My wife will buy most items at one store and then go to another just to buy strawberries because she thought the price of strawberries at the first store was out of line. In a million years, I would never exhibit that kind of behavior.

Allegiance: Men tend to be more brand loyal than women. Women look for the best deal, the most information, the practical aspects of a product or service. Quality and top-notch customer service go a long way with women. Whoever has the highest standards gets their business. There is, however, a big exception. When it comes to financial services providers, women are more brand loyal. If they have a bad experience or if investment performance is weaker than expected, they are less likely to switch from one company to another.

Philanthropy: Americans are a very generous bunch who collectively give away billions of dollars each year to a variety of charities. Yet it is often the women who stand out. It has been proven over and over that the absolute best prospect for almost all not-for-profit organizations is a single, widowed woman over age 60. Still, women of all ages, single, married, divorced, or widowed, have a soft spot for those less fortunate than themselves.

Men, on the other hand, dominate in charitable giving in three specific categories: colleges, environmental groups, and politicians.

As alumni, men tend to stay in close touch with classmates, school news, and particularly with school sports. They prize their alma mater and are interested in its continued stature as a quality center for learning. If a college maintains its academic and athletic excellence, its diplomas retain their value.

Environmental groups find strong support among men who are active in a variety of outdoor sports and recreation. Every year, 20 million men pay for hunting licenses and 60 million for fishing licenses. Without abundant, unspoiled land and clear streams and brooks, there would be no hunting and fishing.

Like the two categories above, contribution to political campaigns are based on practical issues. For the most part, politics heavily affects business, from tax issues to industry legislation. Men still dominate the business landscape and have the strongest desire to support politicians with their wallets, not just their attitudes.

Recreation: Without a doubt men are more sports crazy than women. Sure, there are plenty of women spectators, but how many would actually go to a game or watch football on TV if not with a father, brother, son, boyfriend, or spouse? Sports marketing is a huge activity in practically every country on earth and is thoroughly male dominated. And the related businesses are numerous: beer and hard liquor, sports drinks and soda, apparel, certain personal care products, and all manner of sporting gear.

Looking good: Women spend countless billions on their appearance, from cosmetics and creams to add-on body parts like hair extensions and artificial eyelashes. And of course there is plastic surgery, which has taken mainstream America by storm after hiding out in Hollywood and New York for most of the twentieth century.

Men are far from immune to vanity's siren call. Faith Popcorn, the well-known and respected trend expert, cited as one of her top predictions of 2003 that men would increasingly spend time and money trying to look better, younger, and fitter. She coined a word for this trend: "manity."

Sure enough, men's care products are expanding their lines, and plastic surgery and hair replacement techniques have never been more popular.

The important truth to remember in this category is that women compete with their female friends for "best-looking" bragging rights. Men just want women, all women, to notice them. Women constantly chat with each other about how women look. Men almost never even think about discussing the appearance of other men. These social behaviors are a fundamental difference between the sexes.

From a marketing standpoint, this simply means that women's beauty products should be positioned in the context of women looking good to other women. Men, on the other hand, want to see their products and procedures in the context of women noticing the end result. The razor manufacturers worldwide understand these principles. In industry commercials women are always shown alone, shaving their legs. Men are shown shaving their faces with at least one admiring, beautiful female nearby.

There are no great revelations in marketing to the sexes that can't be explained by their natural chemistry. But it does pay to remember the effect these differences have on behavior and attitude toward a product or service and what targeted message is necessary to attract one or both of the sexes.

15

The Big Breakthrough Idea: Where Does It Come From?

BIG IDEAS OFTEN COME from individuals free enough from day-to-day responsibilities to have a chance to think. No meetings, no phone calls, no normal business chitchat. This does not mean "thinkers" should sit in their offices for eight hours straight. Instead, they should free up their brains and perhaps engage in nonoffice activity: window shopping, more time at Starbucks, a few hours in the back pew of a quiet church—all of which this author has done from time to time.

Steve Ross, the very successful former CEO of Time Warner, used to tell his executive-level employees that if he ever walked into their offices unannounced and found them with their legs propped on the desk, just thinking, he would give them an on-the-spot bonus. His rationale: "I'm paying senior people to think about how to make this company better, not to run the day-to-day business. Anybody can do that."

Not everyone can hit intellectual pay dirt all by themselves. Brainstorming in small groups, where you can bounce ideas off others, can be very effective, especially with the following ground rules.

- First, make sure the group is small, preferably five or six people.
- Second, work with a clear-cut assignment such as solving a major problem or coming up with a way to dramatically increase sales, customer satisfaction, or employee retention.
- Third, limit the assignment to a short time frame, maybe a week or two. Forget about pouring through data for six months, or commissioning special research.
- Fourth, isolate the group from day-to-day business, ideally in a meeting place well away from their usual work environment.

One of the best stories about small group BIG IDEA thinking comes from the wonderful world of Disney. Back in the days when Disneyland had a single California location, Walt Disney decided to expand the Disney Park business to Orlando, Florida. Sounded good, except that Disneyland did not generate nearly enough cash to finance this grand scheme. What's more, Walt was totally opposed to borrowing from banks and going into debt—a throwback to growing up in the Depression and a major distrust of being beholden to bankers.

In a quandary, he called six managers into his office and told them about his vision: to build a bigger, better Disneyland in Florida. Their assignment was to figure out how to finance this very expensive project from the existing business. Walt insisted the group isolate themselves from all contact with their peers and families, and report back to him with an answer on a specific date. He also made it abundantly clear that he did not want to be disappointed. With a sense that he was running out of time, Walt gave them two weeks to come up with a solution.

Two weeks later the managers resurfaced in Walt's office. They had a one-sentence big idea solution: keep Disneyland open at night.

Prior to the meeting, Disneyland routinely closed every evening at 6:00. Their recommendation was to extend evening hours to midnight and promote the evening period as a perfect setting for group outings, such as conventions and tour groups.

We all know what happened. The additional funds poured in and bigger, better Disneyworld was built.

For sure, big payoff ideas should be rewarded. In Walt's case, a couple of weeks after the team of six reported back, they awoke one Saturday morning to find brand-new red Corvette convertibles sitting in their driveways with the keys in an envelope and a handwritten card from the boss. Yes, Walt also paid the taxes for each car by upping the team members' salaries the necessary amount.

To be successful, big ideas must be simple to understand and simple to implement. Like the Disneyland example, they usually entail altering the existing business in a way no one ever considered.

Sometimes the idea is one that makes your product or service break out of the pack and become noticed. Maybe it is a spokesperson who captures the imagination of potential customers. Or a new feature or benefit that really gives you an upper hand with competitors. Yes, others may follow your lead with a similar strategy, but you got there first and that has big impact in any marketplace. Big ideas are all about being first.

Another example of breakthrough thinking is the Vietnam Memorial in Washington, D.C. Instead of selecting a monument that reflected the usual take on war, the team of veterans who ran an intense design competition opted for a radical representation, so extreme that it almost did not get built. There were the usual suspects—soldiers in various states of agony, a big mausoleum-type structure with eagles guarding the entrance, even an oversized GI helmet with an interior covered with soldiers' dog tags.

What was not expected was the power of a black granite slab as envisioned by Maya Ying Lin, the Asian-American graduate student from Yale School of Architecture. Situated below ground level, the sleek memorial dramatically lists the names of all soldiers fallen in battle. Visitors walk downward along the memorial wall, passing names of thousands of soldiers etched into the granite. Eventually, you walk back up to street level as the list comes to an end. The Vietnam Memorial is unlike any war memorial ever built, radically different, highly controversial, and very powerful.

Breakthrough ideas are all about thinking differently. Most are risky at some level and often are not immediately endorsed by the ultimate decision makers.

Of course, sometimes big ideas come from the ultimate decision maker. Probably the most fascinating and brilliant individual I've worked with is Edward "Ned" Johnson, the unquestioned force behind the success of Fidelity Investments. What makes Ned so special is his core belief that people deserve better service than they get. Ned expanded this commitment to better service beyond Fidelity to start two new businesses: Boston Coach, a worldwide limousine service, and the Seaport Hotel, adjacent to Boston's World Trade Center.

Ned started Boston Coach because he was tired of dirty cabs with drivers only vaguely aware of how to get to the desired destination. He was also uncomfortable with traditional limousine service, which was too pretentious for his taste. Thus, Boston Coach was born and shaped around Ned's rules of the road:

1 Provide comfortable cars, not showy limousines
2 Keep each car spotless at all times
3 Have a customer service mentality second to none, with a comprehensive twenty-four-hour customer service center
4 Institute a rigorous driver-training program and immediately sack any drivers who cannot meet ongoing tests on directions, punctuality, politeness, and personal grooming
5 No money will ever change hands between passenger and driver. All charges are billed.
6 Tipping is forbidden. Drivers will be fired for a single infraction.
7 Drivers can participate in profit sharing

Boston Coach became an overnight sensation in Boston and has since expanded to major cities across the United States and abroad.

The Seaport Hotel has a working philosophy similar to Boston Coach's. Spotless rooms, superbly trained and appointed staff, and no tipping. That's right, a hotel where you don't need a roll of small bills to walk in or out, ask for a cab, or get help with your luggage or service from the concierge.

Most companies are founded on an original breakthrough idea: Diner's Club, the first charge card, followed by American Express, Federal Express, Eastern Airlines New

York/Washington/Boston shuttle service, and so on. The list is endless.

A favorite example of a nineteenth-century breakthrough idea is the advent of scheduled shipping. In 1804, a New York City shipping firm was the first to realize that customers would be better served if they knew when to expect goods shipped to them. For thousands of years prior to this big idea, ships were not scheduled. They left port when the captain decided, or when all the cargo holds were full, or the weather turned favorable, or when the crew finally sobered up. This one idea was a HUGE change for world commerce.

One of the most critical roles of a marketing executive is to create an environment where breakthrough ideas, like these, get aired. Where no idea is too crazy to be immediately ruled out. There are many more big ideas out there. Be receptive.

The Web:
Hype and Hope

LIKE ANY OTHER PART of your business, your website can be a critical element in boosting sales and profitability, as long as you understand who you maintain it for—your best customers. If you can delight your best customers with ease of use and total reliability, the two most critical elements in user satisfaction, word of mouth will help build traffic and business.

The belief that a business can lure prospects with a great website is naive. Why? Because the math just doesn't bear out that belief.

In 2000, Forrester Research, the highly regarded technology consulting firm, did a comprehensive study of time spent on the Internet versus watching television. The researchers found that, on average, adults over the age of 18 spend a few minutes a day on the Web as opposed to seven hours a day watching television. They also discovered that Web users frequently visit no more than eleven sites out of the 30 million readily accessible. It also came as no surprise that when watching television, viewers regularly select programs from only eleven channels out of the seventy channels available in most homes. The math is startling: seven hours a day of television versus minutes a day on the Internet. Television is clearly the elephant in the room. Despite the fact that the number of homes with an Internet connection has surpassed the number of homes with cable, the usage statistics are still DRAMATICALLY skewed toward television viewership. Ironically, the millions and millions of available websites work against any one site dominating. Humans have time for only so much data gathering on the Internet.

So how do you make an impact with the Internet deck stacked so solidly against getting noticed? Here's a simple idea to get started. The Internet address of the majority of websites is positioned as an afterthought in promotional literature, advertising, company signage, even on business cards. If you look hard enough, you can usually find it quietly placed at the bottom of the page in very small type. This positioning certainly does not shout COME TO MY WEBSITE!

And that's what it takes. You need to SHOUT. Your Web address should be up front, highly visible, and in large type, so that it visually says, "Come visit right away and good things will happen." Why does nobody do this? Beats me. Think of your Web address as a headline, all by itself. Don't put it in a corner. Don't put it in skinny type. Put it in lights.

Unfortunately, once people are drawn to your site, their first response is likely to be disappointment. Remember the "enemy." When you turn on television, the screen is filled with people in action—newscasters, sports figures, entertainers, soap opera stars—and you are immediately drawn in. Go to practically any website and if there is any motion at all, it is usually some kind of ad for another service. What is often missing is people. And like *People* magazine's avid readers, your website visitors are looking for a way to connect, hoping to meet people who can help them buy or purchase your service.

Online dating services have become popular in large part because people meeting people is their sole product. This is an interesting notion to think about when designing your site. What about a greeter, perhaps an animated character, to welcome visitors and guide them to the content they are looking for? At the very least, there should be a short welcome from the CEO, founder, or company spokesperson.

We all heard the Internet hype of the '90s: television was dead, physical stores were history, and online was the cure for all human needs. Well, that trendy thinking ran its course and emptied many pockets along the way.

All that said, online sites continue to make steady progress in building traffic and business in two major areas: up-to-the-minute news, including financial news; and companies in which simple transactions are done much more easily than by any other non-Web method.

Online banking has been around for over a decade but started to gather steam only in the last few years. Why? It is easy, convenient, and super quick. Nevertheless, this acceptance is limited to simple transactions like checking balances, ordering checks, and looking at online statements. Bill paying online has been a tougher sell because it requires involvement by other parties and just isn't as simple as writing a check and sealing an envelope.

Online travel reservations, or ordering movie or theatre or sports tickets, are online no-brainers that gain in popularity every day. The same is true for online reservations at restaurants locally, or in many major cities and resort areas nationwide.

Online brokerage has been in use for quite some time because it is actually a very simple transaction to buy or sell a stock or mutual fund. With online, you can do it anytime, day or night, efficiently and inexpensively.

The reason for this growing acceptance is clear. Quick, no hassle, instant confirmation, total convenience 24/7. These are the attributes that spell success for online brokers, travel and ticket services, Amazon, eBay, and others in the business of transforming what was once time-consuming and complex. Simple transactions from start to finish. No lines to stand in. No wait time on the telephone. No rejection at the other end of the phone for that dinner reservation you really want.

What does the future hold for the Web, and can it affect our lives in a dramatic and positive fashion? The answer is a resounding yes. Simplification of time-consuming, complex tasks is the grand slam that the Web contributes to anyone connected. Instant communication across town, across country, across continents is a marketer's dream come true.

This then is the hope: that the Internet will become a major engine for international communication and commerce, a true global village for different cultures to better understand each other. Television delivers on many of the same fronts, but not in a truly personal way. You cannot interact directly, the way you can on the Web. The next challenge is to add a dose of the power of TV—its motion and sequencing—to the Web. This final missing ingredient will help realize the Web's true potential going forward and will provide endless creative opportunities for everyone in the marketing profession.

17

The Power of Public Relations and Sponsorships

THERE IS A LOT OF DEBATE among veteran marketers about the effectiveness of advertising versus public relations, as if you must choose one over the other. This is a silly argument—kind of like trying to prove that cancer prevention is better than a cancer cure. You need both applications and always will because they feed off each other, complement each other, need each other. The same is true for advertising and public relations.

PR comes in three basic forms—internal, external, and if you are a public company, investor relations. All three should be well-managed and cultivated, and most important, closely aligned with your overall strategic plan and marketing program. Think of PR as another marketing tool and house it in the marketing group so that it gets the attention it deserves and is always a part of every marketing effort.

Many companies utilize PR only as a reactive measure to deal with bad publicity or the inevitable crisis. Expertise in crisis management is critical, but the ability to be proactive will maximize your PR power. You should always look for ways to put your company in the best possible light. This is not the time to sit around and think good opportunities will just reveal themselves. As Vince Lombardi said, "The best defense is a good offense." Be proactive.

Your first and most important proactive task is to take internal communications seriously and put money into this activity. At a minimum, make internal PR the sole activity of a single staff person; in a small company, this job can be shared.

No company is successful without highly motivated and knowledgeable employees. For years, psychologists have said the top three issues most important to employees are:

1 Recognition
2 Treatment as an insider
3 Appropriate compensation

Note money is third on the list.

You need to communicate with your employees all the time. ALWAYS give them a heads up on the launch of a new marketing campaign. ALWAYS ask for their feedback. ALWAYS alert them to stories about to appear in the press, both positive and negative. ALWAYS communicate with them as equals. Senior executives must be able and willing to meet with employees regularly and talk frankly about the good, the bad, and the ugly aspects of the business.

After employees, your second most important audience is the journalists who cover your industry. Again, senior and even middle management should be accessible. In most cases they need coaching and media training to really become effective advocates of your firm. There are a few "naturals" out there but they are the exceptions. Make sure a PR professional is always present when a reporter talks to an employee of any rank, on the telephone or in person. This third-party presence helps keep everyone on the straight and narrow.

Treat reporters with respect and dignity. Do not act arrogant or too busy to answer questions. In fact, you should thank them for spending their valuable time with you.

I remember a reporter from a major business publication who called me on background about a Fortune 50 CEO who I used to work for. The reporter said his publication planned to run a major story on how well this CEO was running the company a year after he had taken the top job. In response to questions, I said this fellow was brilliant, occasionally impatient with others, but deep down a decent individual who really cared about the company, the employees, and its customers.

A few weeks later the reporter called to thank me for the background and said that the upcoming article about the CEO would be exceedingly negative. Three reasons: the CEO kept the reporter waiting for an hour; during the interview, the CEO said he had more important things to do and could only spend half the time that had been promised; to add insult to injury, the CEO then said he didn't think much of reporters to begin with.

This story shows that really smart leaders can do really dumb things when representing their company. Where were the PR professionals who should have coached this CEO long ago about how to win reporters over?

Relationships with the media need to be cultivated and managed in the best interests of the company. This is not manipulation in any way, just basic good manners.

The first step in managing this relationship is to learn a little about reporters. In general, they are a group of smart people, well-educated but not necessarily well-rounded. They usually feel underpaid and underappreciated by their own organization. A cynical bunch, they make significantly less money than the people they report on and often resent that fact. And like most people under pressure, will cut corners to make a story deadline.

Here are some tips on how to deal with reporters:

- Always call back promptly, even if you can't help them
- Try to give exclusive coverage to two or three key industry reporters on a rotating basis
- Always be on time for interviews
- Always request the ability to check facts before a story goes to print
- If there is a point you really want to make, repeat it several times during an interview—in fact, keep repeating it until you are sick of saying it
- Regardless of what you are promised, you are always "on the record"
- Buy them lunch occasionally and thank them for covering your business

What about investor relations? Companies can improve their image with the offer of regular access to senior executives via conference calls and Web content. Ask for shareholder opinion—all the time. On your website. In your annual report. On a special inbound automated phone number exclusively for shareholder use. These folks will always tell it like it is—good, bad, whatever. Every once in a while, you may even get a REALLY good idea.

And don't forget to acknowledge comments promptly. While you are at it, why not have a special product or service offer available only to shareholders. If companies spent more time making shareholders feel special, they might discover a significant source of additional business. Think shareholder marketing instead of shareholder relations. You may not be blood relations, but you do share an interest in the growth of a successful business.

Sponsorships

Let's not beat around the bush. Sponsorships are controversial. Does the Macy's Thanksgiving Day Parade generate additional business for Macy's? Did the Fleet Center in Boston do anything for Fleet Bank or Bank of America, its parent company? What about Exxon Mobil's long-running sponsorship of Masterpiece Theatre? The list goes on and on and on.

It is almost impossible to calculate the effect of sponsorships on a company's bottom line. If you are solely focused on increased revenue, then sponsorships are not for you. But if you consider other ways to measure its value, such as the very positive impact it can have on employees and their families, sponsorship can be extremely rewarding.

A timeless story, Charles Dickens's *A Christmas Carol* may be one of the first literary examples of sponsorship and its payback. Ebenezer Scrooge viewed everything in precise monetary terms until his night with the ghosts of Christmas past, present, and future. Then, following a revelation that money for money's sake was not such a cool pursuit after all, he essentially sponsored Tiny Tim and the Cratchet family for the rest of his days. His reward? It just made him feel good.

Integration is key to a successful sponsorship. And please pardon the pun, as I relate my experience with Key Corp and Key Arena in Seattle.

In the mid-1990s, as chief marketing officer at Key Corp I engineered their sponsorship of Seattle's brand new basketball arena. Although Key Corp is headquartered in Cleveland, it has a significant banking presence in Washington, most notably in the Seattle area.

The owners of the Seattle Sonics approached Key Corp about a fifteen-year sponsorship of the new arena scheduled to open in 1997. The annual sponsorship cost was around $1.1 million, and as these things go, a reasonable sum. Although it had been in Seattle for eight years, Key Bank's awareness level via consumer research was in single digits. It was clear that this sponsorship was a way to dramatically boost the awareness of Key Bank in the Seattle market.

To cut to the chase, we put together a totally integrated marketing package in order to convince Key Corp's CEO and its Board that our business in the Northwest would clearly benefit from this union. The deal was done.

Key Bank's major competitor, SeaFirst, with nearly 100 percent awareness, had been the sponsor of the old basketball arena. People at SeaFirst were none too happy when they learned we had signed the new sponsorship right under their noses. Ironically, SeaFirst had ATM rights for the adjacent Space Needle Park area, including the grounds outside the basketball arena—but not the arena itself. Talk about fun and high intrigue.

Yes, beating SeaFirst out of the new arena sponsorship was a huge coup. But as the previous sponsor, why didn't SeaFirst have a leg up? Simply put, they took a long-standing relationship for granted.

When plans were announced for the new arena, including the availability of naming rights, SeaFirst just assumed that they would be the sponsor. They did not sit down with all parties to immediately work out a new arrangement, and their inaction miffed the Sonics management. Enter Key Corp, which was ready to negotiate and quickly work out an agreement—not in weeks or months, but days. This speedy decision making was the clincher. If you are keen to go after a potential sponsorship and know other parties might be in the running, go for immediate closure. Cut everyone else off at the pass. There is no reason for a long courtship in this kind of relationship before the two parties get married.

Now it was time to name the new arena. Both governing bodies, the city of Seattle and the SuperSonics management, thought it should be called Key Bank Arena. Not such a classy option, a little too self-serving, and an inaccurate representation of Key Corp's other businesses with names like Champion Mortgage and McDonald's Investments. In the end, we opted for Key Arena. Simple and dignified. The local press was thrilled that the word "bank" was omitted from their brand-new world-class basketball arena. Clearly, a good move for Key Corp and the Seattle community.

In the first six months of the sponsorship, Key Bank's awareness in the Seattle market went from about 8 percent to 50 percent. It continued to head north from there and after two years was on a par with SeaFirst.

Stadium arrangements are complicated. If you have never done one of these deals before, make sure you hire a consultant or attorney who has. As a point of reference, listed below are the main points of Key Corp's fifteen-year marketing agreement with Seattle's basketball arena:

- Four-sided rooftop sign with arena name, illuminated at night
- Signs at all main entrances to the arena, including the attached parking garage
- Significant signage on the basketball floor and exclusive ownership of the scoring box atop the basketball floor
- Key's logo on all uniformed stadium personnel, on all napkins, plates, dishes, and plastic cups used by vendors within the arena
- Exclusive ATM rights within the arena
- A special branch at one corner of the arena
- A center court suite seating twenty—available for all events in the arena, basketball or otherwise
- Access to mailing lists of all suite and season ticket holders
- Key's logo and name on all tickets for all events held at the arena
- On televised games, the Key logo to appear at each commercial break
- Free commercial time on local radio and television covering each home or away game of the Seattle Sonics
- A block of half-price tickets for Key employees and their families for all Sonics home games
- First right of refusal to sponsor any other events of any nature to be held at Key Arena during the fifteen-year term
- In the event of a basketball strike, a prorated credit on the annual sponsorship cost

Politics and Promotion

WHEN YOU THINK ABOUT IT, political campaigns employ all the elements of marketing success due to their pivotal concentration on one particular point in time—Election Day. Nothing else is more important than the election of the candidate on that day.

Every element of a successful political campaign is magnified and simplified at the same time. With Election Day as an end point, there is no time and no interest in endless debate on budgets, strategy, message testing, media planning and replanning. What's more, political campaigns engender evershrinking consumer attention spans.

Consequently, the campaign team must get focused. Stay focused. Build excitement. Create positive news about the candidate. Have a compelling call to action—why folks out there should vote for their candidate. And do it all with an immovable deadline.

During a political campaign, all the tools of marketing come into play—from the creation of a unique selling proposition and a good tag line to knowledge of the voting "customer," the use of public relations, special events, public speaking, and of course, the candidate's memorable and distinctive personality. Marketers can learn a lot from the pressure cooker environment of a political campaign. At some point, make sure you volunteer time to work for a public candidate. Politics is marketing, through and through.

Back in the '70s and '80s, I worked on direct marketing campaigns for several candidates and national party organizations such as the Republican Senatorial Committee. During that time, I met Paul Newman, an extremely savvy political consultant. Not Butch Cassidy, he is a little paunchy, has brown eyes, and always refers to himself as "the real Paul Newman."

Paul's simple philosophy of how to run successful political campaigns applies to any marketing activity.

1   Forget the term, "voter." People don't wake up in the morning, look in the mirror, and say, "Gee, I am happy that I am a voter." Actually, voters do not think about your candidate, or any candidate, much at all.

In business, we mistakenly believe that consumers think of themselves as customers of our enterprise. They do, but only very occasionally, when they have a specific need or a problem that we can help solve.

2   Voter apathy means people are basically satisfied, not that they do not appreciate their freedom and their country. In the same way, your customers will not call every day to say, "Thanks for being in business. I really appreciate it." That does not mean they are indifferent to your product or service.

3 According to Paul, political campaigns boil down to "meatball surgery." The last three weeks of a political campaign are the whole ball game. You have to pull out all the stops, blast the airwaves, and campaign nonstop. This is when people may actually pay attention to all the rhetoric in the media. These three weeks are the time when people begin to realize that there is a candidate they may indeed vote for on a rapidly approaching Election Day.

In business, every marketing letter, ad, brochure, and campaign should have a deadline—a clear reason for a consumer to respond within a relatively short time frame.

4 People truly think of themselves as voters only when they walk into the voting booth. And then their decision is: "Do I vote for Nitwit A or Nitwit B?"

In business, the belief that there are major points of difference between your product and the other guy's is often not perceived by the consumer. Is the message clear about what makes you special, and better, and thus the right "candidate" for the consumer vote? Stay in touch with your constituency. If all you read is the *New York Times* or the *Wall Street Journal,* you are guaranteed to be out of touch with mainstream America. Subscribe to one or two small-town newspapers, separate from where you grew up.

RightTime Marketing

Back in the early '90s, I coined the term RightTime Marketing. It means getting the right message to the right individual at exactly the right time. A very logical marketing principle and easy to remember, but it takes a lot of precision and attention to detail to pull off. It can be the ultimate "tipping point" in political campaigns.

One of my first political clients, Mayor Kevin White of Boston, was running for an unprecedented fourth term and was concerned about voter fatigue. Together with his local political consultant, we devised a plan to make sure Mayor White delivered a powerful message of caring to voting districts where past elections had shown voter apathy to be a real problem.

Three months before Election Day, volunteers campaigned door-to-door in the targeted districts. They asked each resident to look at a short list of ten issues and select three that were the most important to him or her. These top three issues were tabulated along with the individual's address. Seven days before the election, we sent out several hundred thousand personalized computer letters from Kevin White to each resident who had spoken with a volunteer.

The letters expressed Mayor White's passion for his job and the City of Boston. They went on to say that if reelected to a fourth term, the top three issues on his agenda would be... the three that the recipient had mentioned several months ago. In essence, the campaign delivered a personalized platform from the mayor to the voters at the key decision-making moment: "Should I vote for Mayor White, for the other guy, or not at all?" The Mayor won with a margin that reflected a much better than expected showing in the districts targeted with this letter campaign.

Here's an example of RightTime Marketing at the national level:

When President Richard Nixon, along with his running mate, Spiro Agnew, formally announced his bid for a second term, the Democratic National Committee wasted no time.

They quickly sent several million registered Democrats a short and very pointed letter. Just seven lines long, it raised a ton of money.

Dear Ms. Nelson,

There are two very important reasons why you should make a special donation today, for as much as you can, to the Democratic National Committee.

1. Richard Nixon
2. Spiro Agnew

Please let me hear from you right away. There is no time to waste.

The very future of America is at stake.

Sincerely
(signed by chairman of committee)

There are many creative ways to get the right message to the right person at the right time, and the payoff can be huge. Think about the opportunities in your business. You might want to refer to Chapter Twelve, where I discuss how to alleviate post-purchase anxiety. This is fundamentally RightTime Marketing in action with every customer, every time they interact with your company.

TV TV TV

The tube is HUGE. I often remind colleagues that to get the attention of the majority of Americans we have to remember the role of TV in their daily lives. All the studies done on TV habits over the past five decades show the consistent presence of TV in our day-to-day existence. On average, every American adult 18 and over watches six to seven hours of television daily. They may not be glued to the set this entire time, but the TV is on, blaring away.

Since the first political campaign TV commercials done by the Eisenhower camp in the early '50s, TV has become the single most important element of getting candidates' messages out to potential voters. The presidential debates every four years are the second most watched shows after the Super Bowl. Leading up to the most recent national election in November 2004, almost $2 billion was spent in the summer and fall of that year on paid political advertising for local and national candidates.

Much of this advertising is what I call "attack the other guy" and it is controversial and always will be. Unfortunately it works. It energizes the supporters of the candidates on both sides, which doesn't really change anything, but it also sways some undecided voters against the candidate under attack. It also keeps other potential voters at home, those who just get turned off by the whole process. In certain elections in certain parts of the country, keeping voters from turning out is an unspoken strategy.

The numbers from the most recent 2004 presidential election point to this fact. A record turnout of 120 million people voted for either George W. Bush or John Kerry. But another

80 million people who were eligible to vote did not—a whopping 40 percent of all eligible voters. During every election campaign period, many people just get fed up with all the negative advertising and do nothing. They subscribe to Paul Newman's Nitwit A versus Nitwit B theory in this way: why vote when I don't like either candidate?

And likeability is key, key, key to winning elections. How a candidate appears on screen is how the vast majority of Americans judge where to place their vote or whether to not vote at all. This is a point worth remembering for those occasions when representatives from your company must appear on TV. You must do everything in your power to help them project a favorable image.

TV was dubbed a cool, meaning cold, medium by Marshall McLuhan, who came to fame in the '50s and the '60s as a guru of the modern communications age. He also referred to the family television as "the electronic fireplace."

What he meant by cool was that it is difficult to appear warm and friendly on camera. The news anchors and morning TV hosts are pros who make it look like no big deal—but it is. Even politicians who spend way more time in front of TV cameras than almost any other group are not all silky smooth on TV—in fact, far from it.

The bottom line is this: To come across well on television you either have to have an engaging personality, which few have, or you have to be a really accomplished actor in terms of projecting yourself in front of a camera so that you appear engaging. One really has to work at it.

Those who succeed in front of a camera have to love it, or appear to love being there. Candidates can't fake it. Certainly your CFO or CEO can't fake it. The person who succeeds in connecting with a TV audience is someone who absolutely loves to face the camera and make a pitch. Love is the right word. A very, very few do this naturally. Most people including politicians appear stiff and unnatural.

Net net, the best spokesperson for your company other than a paid actor is a senior-level employee who is willing to spend long hours polishing her performance in front of a camera and work with a professional coach some of the time.

In the Spotlight

THE OPPORTUNITIES to speak in front of a group come early, and most of us started the same way—Show and Tell in kindergarten. Remember how much we enjoyed it, even without slides, PowerPoint, and video? Unfortunately, somewhere along the way to adulthood, many people acquire a fear of public speaking. In fact, it is on the top ten list of phobias, causing anxiety, panic, and a dogged determination to avoid making presentations at any cost.

If you are among those who dread public speaking—get over it. You cannot be an effective marketing professional without the ability and passion to make your case forcefully to groups that range in size from one or two others to a full auditorium.

You must always be able to convince people that a percentage of your company's hard-earned revenue should be diverted to marketing programs, often with no immediate payback. What your listeners buy, in essence, is you. They buy your ability to make things happen. All the great marketing ideas in the world don't mean squat if you can't articulate them, usually with little advance notice, to everyone from your own assistant to the CEO you get five minutes with twice a year.

While I do not have a cure for the fear of public speaking, I do have some tips that will help improve your skills.

• Know your material through and through. Practice your talk and then practice some more. And when you think you have practiced enough, do it again. Very few people are naturally gifted speakers. Think of public speaking as a sport that you are trying to get really good at. You have to do it a lot. Most people are nervous because they have not done it much and in fact avoid public speaking whenever they can. The right approach is just the opposite. Public speaking must become second nature to you. And that will only happen if you get up on your feet as often as the opportunity presents itself.

• Most of the time, reading a speech word for word is not the right approach. Although it may feel more comfortable to you, your audience will usually be bored silly. A better approach is to use 3"x5" index cards, bulleted with the major points you want to cover. Do not be afraid to hold these cards in your hands. You can walk around a stage with them—even throw them on the floor one by one as you proceed through your talk, kind of like David Letterman throwing his Top Ten cards out the window every night. It is good to show some flair and not take yourself too seriously. Hand-held cards are versatile and work with any size group, from 20 to 2,000.

● A good way to get into the groove of public speaking is to start with a small group around a table. You can even sit among them. This is generally a pretty comfortable setting for most people. After some practice, you might want to stand at the end of the table. When you gain some more confidence, you can move up to a podium or stage setting. Go slowly and stay relaxed. Little steps make for great strides.

● I get asked a lot about how to use a stage. Should you stand behind the podium or walk around or do both? The answer is, it depends. Each room is different. Sometimes you have to stand behind the podium because the microphone is attached or lighting is only centered on the podium area. As a speaker you need to get comfortable with the setting. Then decide what works best. When in doubt just stand behind the podium. No one is going to remember your talk based on where you stood. If the President of the United States almost always uses a podium, why not you?

● Whenever possible, visit the assigned speaking venue several hours before your talk and check it out thoroughly. If you have audiovisual aids, meet with the on-site technical people and do a thorough rundown of your requirements ahead of time. These people know what they are doing. They can handle pretty much anything you can throw at them, given some lead time.

● Always bring a couple of backup copies of your presentation, even if you sent it ahead of time. Never assume anything got to where it was supposed to go.

● Yes, PowerPoint and slide presentations are very popular—from a speaker's point of view, not necessarily that of the audience. The majority of these presentations are chockfull of charts, graphs, figures, and endless bullet points, most of which serve only one unintended purpose—to bore your audience beyond belief. All these visual aids are just crutches. If you want to be mediocre, like many speakers, then use the crutches. If not, drop most of the visual aids. Use a few slides with a few words in large type. Think of each slide as a headline, as a major point you want to discuss. Pictures of the person, place, or item you want to describe are fine, too. And quick video clips can help keep your audience involved.

● If you show video clips, insert seven-second spacing to give your audience time to absorb one clip and get ready to watch the next. This spacing also allows you to set up the next clip with a few words to tune your audience in to what they are about to see.

● When in doubt, cut it out. If you are asked to speak for thirty minutes, practice a talk that takes fifteen. This is not easy to do, but is essential to a solid presentation. It will allow you to speak at a slower pace and increase your chances of connecting with the audience. The biggest mistakes speakers make are to talk way too fast and cover far too much material. The net effect is a speech that the listener is unable follow. One way to slow yourself down and prevent motor mouth is to write PAUSE after each section of your talk, and do that before you move on to the next point. When I first started to do a lot of public speaking, this technique was especially effective. Eventually you will be able to drop the reminder, but it is good training for a beginner.

● Speaking is acting, plain and simple. And just like theater, enthusiasm and animation are requisite to gain and maintain an audience's attention. Whether you use note cards or speak from text, write the words HIGH ENERGY at the very top of the first card or page of your talk. You need to be up and energetic throughout your entire presentation. That energy will spread among your audience. Notice how sea-soned politicians or very good preachers can fire up a group. A lot has to do with the speaker's high energy level.

● To really make a point, say the sentence or phrase, pause, and say it again. This technique of repetition is power-ful and should be used sparingly in your talk.

● Never have a long laundry list of points, as in "I will be discussing the following ten points over the next hour." Your audience will immediately hope someone yells "FIRE" in the auditorium. Stick with smaller numbers, as in "I will cover four major reasons why we must change the way we do busi-ness around the globe."

Franklin Roosevelt was once asked about guidelines for making presentations. He said there are three basic rules: walk to the podium and smile, get to the point, sit down.

Probably the best advice is to hire a speech coach for a few sessions. This will be money well spent to make you a more effective speaker the rest of your life.

In the Hot Seat

Being interviewed for a job or responding to a reporter is not all that different from public speaking. You need to have high energy. You need to speak slowly. You need to repeat a sen-tence now and then for emphasis, and you need to pause.

Unlike a presentation where you already know what you want to say, an interview can catch you off guard. You listen to a question and then formulate a response. Not so easy. The age-old technique of repeating a question to buy time is fine if not overdone.

Whether you interview for a job or respond to questions for an article in the local paper, always assume you are on the record. Period. Never say anything you would not like to see in print or hear on the air. There just is no such thing as "off the record," especially in today's world.

With reporters, it is always best to think of yourself as on the witness stand. That does not mean you should be stiff or unsmiling. Most of the time, the best answer to any question is a short and direct answer. Do not ramble on and try to over-explain—it just makes you look defensive.

On occasion, you may be asked to be interviewed for a television program or segment. This usually entails a visit to a local studio where you wear an earplug, look into a camera, and are not face-to-face with the interviewer who is in some distant facility. This is often how live television interviews are done and can be very disconcerting to a novice. You will have just a few seconds, usually no more than thirty, to make your point and there are no second chances.

What to do? Really nothing more than know your topic cold and come to the interview with rehearsed, quick, to-the-point answers. With these types of interviews, you will be given the basic questions in advance. If you wind up with a face-to-face interview, the segment will be longer. In either situation, you must practice, practice, practice. Unless you are a veteran this is NOT the time to wing it. And remember my favorite two words for all public speakers: HIGH ENERGY.

It is essential to stay focused on the interviewer, despite the cameras. Ignore the red lights and forget they are there. Assume you are on camera from the minute you walk onto the set until the minute you leave. Do not put your hands in embarrassing places until you are far, far away from the set.

Speaking of hands, men more than women are guilty of the "fig leaf" pose. Even seasoned politicians occasionally lapse into this position. Avoid the gesture at all times. It is a weak and lame position and makes anyone look pathetic. Instead, think of yourself as Captain Bligh in any of the three movie versions of *Mutiny on the Bounty*. He walks the deck with his hands firmly clasped behind his back. Now that is the posture of a leader.

Confucius and Stardom

MARKETING STARS create big ideas that work. And they come up with them because they have the time to think.

"The busy man is never able. The able man is never busy."

Confucius allegedly said this in the fourth century B.C., and Time Warner's Steve Ross knew it when he rewarded any executive he caught thinking. Thinking is what every marketing professional should strive for. You will never be a marketing star if you don't take the time to contemplate, conjure, and dream.

Many marketing professionals measure success by their number of direct reports, the total head count in the marketing department, and by the size of their marketing budget.

Headhunters encourage this analysis with their insistence that these criteria somehow measure one's ability. In truth, a better barometer would be how successful you are in the creation of compelling new ways to grab customers' attention, excite them, and get them to buy more, year after year.

To become a marketing star, you have to know how to inspire and manage people. You have to come up with ideas that they can get behind, ideas that will significantly move the business needle. You do not need them to report to you. Remember, ideas are budget-free until they are put into action. If an idea is compelling and good enough to impact the business, at some point the higher-ups will get you the bucks to give it a try. If not, come up with another one and keep at it.

Like Thomas Edison, all great idea people fail, fail, and fail again before success comes their way. Invention by its very nature is a series of mistakes or seemingly wrong paths taken that eventually lead to a positive outcome. Why should marketing be any different?

If you don't want to think and experiment and tinker and doodle and think some more about how to get customers to love you and buy more, you may still deserve to be somewhere on the marketing team, but you will never be the star.

There is a reason why a submarine captain has an executive officer who runs every aspect of day-to-day operations. The captain's job is not to run the boat. It is to inspire the crew, to think of how to make their jobs more productive, to think of better ways for the boat to operate. It is also to inspire confidence, boost morale, and encourage the crew to make the boat's performance the very best it can be.

The number one job of senior marketing professionals is to recruit the best second in command they can possibly find.

Sweating the Details

To some degree, and very often to a large degree, the success of any marketing effort is directly related to the correct fulfillment of your product or service to the customer. For every marketing promotion, an individual on your internal staff should be assigned to sweat the details of fulfillment. It is not enough to rely on an outside service, especially one that is miles or continents away from your offices.

You need a professional who is accountable to you. It should also be someone who loves the challenge and science of what happens from the time an order is placed to the time you get an acknowledgment of receipt by the customer.

Your fulfillment expert should be highly motivated, and highly rewarded for a job well done.

The number two job is to let the second in command run the ship so that they can do the creative thinking needed to leapfrog your competitors.

All of this requires a work environment that encourages free thinking and fresh initiative. When I'm asked what a marketing professional should look for in a job, the size of your company's marketing department or how many direct reports you will have is not my first response. What I do say is:

Do you have really good chemistry with your potential boss and colleagues?

Will you get the latitude to do the job of transforming the company's marketing from okay to great? After all, why take a job just to do okay marketing?

Is there commitment to spend the money if great ideas are forthcoming?

Pretty simple rules of engagement. And remember, being able is way better than being busy—for you and your company.

How to Make the Most
of Your Advertising Agency

BACK IN THE '70S AND '80S, the glory days of advertising, agencies were driven primarily by creative superstars, totally passionate about the power of applying their imagination to a marketing challenge. Some of the best advertising of all time was produced during that period. Then in the '90s, agencies went public and people passionate about numbers replaced creatives as captains of the industry. It took only a few more years before the numbers-driven titans began gobbling up smaller shops and cannibalizing each other. The result is today's mega-agency, big, bigger, biggest.

This shift in agency structure means that it is more important than ever to properly manage that relationship. How you handle your agency will determine whether you will get the very best product from their collective creative minds. Yes, there is still a lot of talent around, but most clients get the advertising they deserve because they manage agency relationships poorly—from ridiculous accusations of supposed conflicts to sucking ALL the risk-taking out of the creative process.

To manage an agency properly, first and foremost there has to be chemistry and trust. All agencies are capable of great work if there is rapport between your staff and theirs and a true feeling of partnership. If there is no connection, find a group you can relate to as fast as you possibly can.

How to measure chemistry?

1   You like exchanging ideas, concerns, hopes, and dreams with the agency folks assigned to you.
2   You enjoy socializing with them.
3   You can completely trust them with confidential information—from the head account person to the summer intern.
4   You believe the agency is genuinely interested in your business.

Next, remember an agency's product is its people. It all boils down to the golden rule—treat your agency team as you would expect to be treated—praise good work and pay for it. If you want to nickel and dime your agency to death then don't expect their best thinking and brightest creatives on your account. Give criticism and make it constructive. Your goal as a client is to be the account that personnel throughout the agency want to be assigned to. That doesn't mean you have to be a pushover who just sits back and lets your agency run the show. Insist on teamwork. Encourage big ideas. Join in brainstorming sessions.

Then there's the money. There is nothing fundamentally wrong with the finance people who have a large say in running today's businesses. But, whether on the agency side or the client side, they don't inspire; they don't create a passion for the business where free thinking flows and big ideas flourish. They are partly the reason why there is so little exceptional marketing and advertising done today.

What to do about it? I actually think we marketers should spend more time talking to our respective finance departments about what we do and how we do it. We need to get them more engaged in how marketing can transform a business and its bottom line. And we should do this in conjunction with our agency team.

Most finance people on the client side never see an agency presentation or ever meet a creative director or media planner. No wonder they are less than thrilled with the bills they see for creative services. It's all extremely undefined for them. Who are these agency people? What makes them worth the money we pay? An occasional face-to-face update with the finance folks can be an eye-opener for both sides.

As for compensation, agencies seem fixated on charging by the hour. I have no problem with this approach insofar as they need to calculate what they pay each employee per hour. But beyond the pure math, this fixation on hours makes no sense.

The creative process does not lend itself to two hours of thinking about problem A and four hours about problem B. Nor does copywriting or layout and design, or even media planning. Creative thinking and inspiration can come at any time: in the middle of the night, over a scotch and soda, during a six-mile jog, while sitting in a boring meeting on a completely different topic.

I don't care how many hours a person punches on the clock during the day. I am paying for their brainpower and the use of a team to do a certain project over a specific period of time. Within that period of time they should feel free to think about my business at any time, in any situation, without worrying about the exact hours they put in on a certain day, or week, or month. Agencies and clients need to remember that the value of a passionate idea or a new visual approach to the business that pops up one evening while walking the dog can't be quantified by an hourly rate. GREAT work comes out of freedom from the day-to-day accounting chores—it really and truly does.

A final piece of advice about agency compensation. The best approach is to agree to a monthly fee that covers all expected work. It should be made clear that there are no extra or hidden charges. If the scope of work changes, either side should be allowed to request a review and the fee should be adjusted accordingly.

A Few Words about Copywriters

You may not be a Hollywood insider, but your awareness of good writing has probably been honed by that industry. Oscar-winning movies like *The Godfather* and *Patton,* or long-running sitcoms like *Fraser* and *Friends,* would not have made it without stellar lines for actors to speak.

Just as in those popular vehicles, copy is the single most important element in any marketing campaign. It is the voice of your product or service and delivers your message. Its impact cannot be underestimated. But just how much is that copy worth, and how do you properly motivate and compensate a copywriter?

173

Most advertising agencies today still bill by the hour, which makes some sense for general management of time, but no sense for creative activities like writing. How long does it take to write a good promotional letter, or print ad campaign, or television script for a thirty-second commercial? Who knows! Sometimes a day, sometimes a week, sometimes fifteen minutes. I have written ads in my head while jogging and on a note pad while waiting for a movie to start. This is a common experience among writers, especially in the marketing world.

Given these unpredictable creative quirks, you should pay by the project and settle up-front on the fee. There are no hard and fast rules. Writers are a funny bunch. Some think they are worth a lot, and some are worth way more than they think. Sometimes just one good line is priceless.

Often the best way to pay an agency, or the writer if he is freelance, is based on a day rate. If the copy gets done in fifteen minutes and is brilliant, why should you care how long it took to create?

A day rate for a seasoned copywriter can run from $2,500 to as much as $10,000. Think Moroccan bazaar and negotiate. For unknown reasons, writers have a desire to bargain. Negotiations with writers usually take place in two dimensions: what they think their day rate should be, and how many days they think the project will take. For most small projects, you should pay for a day or two of their time. For a major multimedia campaign, you might consider a flat monthly fee for one to three months.

Once you agree to a price, and don't be afraid to be tough, you should surprise the writer the next day by offering to add a bit more to the fee. Nothing makes writers feel better than the belief that you spent time thinking their work was actually worth more than you originally agreed. I know this sounds silly, but it really works. Like creatives in any field, writers are insecure and have a high need for approval: "How did I do? How did I do?" This thought is always on their minds. Make them feel great and they will work harder to please you and create something really special.

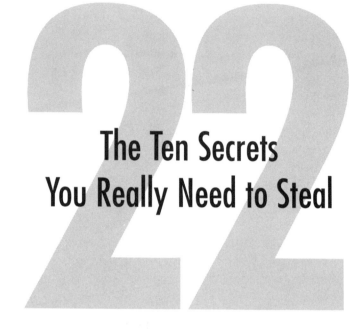

The Ten Secrets
You Really Need to Steal

OKAY, YOU DON'T WANT to read this whole book. Or better yet, you read it and want to rip out a couple of pages that will remind you of the critical stuff as you debut as a marketing star in your large business, small business, or not-for-profit group.

These top ten secrets are not ranked in order of importance. They are all equally important.

● **Three essential marketing ingredients.** Successful marketing campaigns have three essential ingredients. They are visually exciting, they create news, and they include a compelling call to action. Together these three elements should stop viewers or readers in their tracks, make them pay attention to the message, and get them to act on it quickly.

● **Brand power is about creating a strong visual connection.** Think the Marlboro cowboy, the glass Coke bottle, Colonel

Sanders, Mr. Clean, and the list goes on. Every successful brand must have a visual or written unique selling proposition that sets the brand apart from competitors and makes it special. This USP should be clear, concise, and completely understood by every single employee and, you hope, millions of customers as well.

● **Don't listen to art directors.** Art directors are dead set against anyone actually reading the ad you spent big bucks to produce. Insist on serif typefaces (type with feet) and overrule the use of white reverse type in any fashion, in any promotion, 98 percent of the time. Long ago, the famous adman David Ogilvy wrote, "The consumer isn't stupid, she's your wife." I would add, "And she's 57 years old and won't read small or hard-to-read type."

● **Emulate *People* magazine.** *People* magazine is the most successful paid-subscription magazine in history. Its success is based on four principles that you can use to create the most compelling marketing materials possible.

1 Use pictures of real people, not models who are nameless

2 Use captions with pictures, always, always, always

3 Write concisely; you are not on a government commission

4 Leave plenty of white space on every page so the eye can digest what's there

● **The power of personality.** There is nothing more powerful than a company spokesperson who is an integral part of your unique selling proposition. This is the number one way to give your product or service the absolute best chance to succeed. Finding the right person or animal or animated character is a critical function that you should take very seriously.

- **There are few customers who really matter.** Remember how few customers actually contribute to your take-home pay. In most businesses, 10 percent of the customers generate 90 percent of the revenue. In the not-for-profit world, typically 1 percent of contributors provide 50 percent of your donations. Do you pay enough attention to these most important customer/donor segments? Your answer should be a resounding "yes," or "I plan to start tomorrow!"

- **The most important customer lesson ever learned.** People renew the way they are acquired. If I liked the first Armani suit I ever wore, chances are I will want another. If I fell in love with a BMW at age 28 and bought one, I will want similar handling and performance in the future. If I think Angelina Jolie is the sexiest woman alive, I will go see every movie she is in. This law of renewal applies across the board to all age groups, in all cultures, from the dawn of time through however long we remain on the planet.

- **Great marketers are great speakers.** You will never become a marketing star if you do not learn to enjoy public speaking. Practically no one is born a natural speaker. Some of the best money you can spend is on the fee to hire a speaking coach for a few months. It will really pay off. And, never, ever do the fig leaf pose, where you stand with your hands in front of your unmentionables. Do not do this in public or for that matter at any waking moment. This pose screams "weak" and "lame" and is guaranteed to make you look pathetic.

- **Customer loyality programs must have a perceived value that exceeds their perceived cost.** Make sure your customer recognition strategy oozes real value. Example: If I pay $500 annually for a premium credit card it's because the benefits I'll receive from its regular use will well exceed those 500 bucks.

- **There are six reasons to advertise** (in order or importance):
1 Motivate your staff and make them feel proud of the company they work for
2 Remind existing customers why they are customers
3 Generate new leads
4 Recruit great people from your competitors
5 Get noticed by the press and gain more awareness from the public in doing so
6 Build the brand. More awareness is always good. A universal truth.

Being All That We Can Be

I HOPE THESE CHAPTERS better your professional knowledge of the craft of marketing.

This book is meant as a reference guide, one that really should never go out of date. Sure, products change, pricing changes, features and fashion and technology change. But human nature really doesn't. Even in years and decades and centuries past, when people ostensibly had more time to think, they still wanted to be sold in a direct and relatively rapid way. No matter what point in time, we move through life with too many things to do and too little time to do them.

We need to use straightforward marketing.

We need to understand what turns people on and gets them to buy products and services.

We need to understand the key elements of building successful brands.

We need to reduce our marketing jargon and stop the endless charts and graphs that no one remembers the next day.

We need big ideas to propel our profession and our companies forward in future years.

We need to learn from past mistakes that have marked this profession since shopkeepers, peddlers, and traders first appeared on the scene, thousands of years ago.

There is really nothing more important for a marketing professional to do than to get the right product in front of the right customer with the least amount of waste in time and money.

Index

About Bloomberg

BLOOMBERG L.P., founded in 1981, is a global information services, news, and media company. Headquartered in New York, the company has sales and news operations worldwide.

Bloomberg, serving customers on six continents, holds a unique position within the financial services industry by providing an unparalleled range of features in a single package known as the BLOOMBERG PROFESSIONAL® service. By addressing the demand for investment performance and efficiency through an exceptional combination of information, analytic, electronic trading, and Straight Through Processing tools, Bloomberg has built a worldwide customer base of corporations, issuers, financial intermediaries, and institutional investors.

BLOOMBERG NEWS®, founded in 1990, provides stories and columns on business, general news, politics, and sports to leading newspapers and magazines throughout the world. BLOOMBERG TELEVISION®, a 24-hour business and financial news network, is produced and distributed globally in seven languages. BLOOMBERG RADIO℠ is an international radio network anchored by flagship station BLOOMBERG® 1130 (WBBR-AM) in New York.

In addition to the BLOOMBERG PRESS® line of books, Bloomberg publishes *BLOOMBERG MARKETS®* and *BLOOMBERG WEALTH MANAGER®* magazines. To learn more about Bloomberg, call a sales representative at:

London:	+44-20-7330-7500
New York:	+1-212-318-2000
Tokyo:	+81-3-3201-8900

FOR IN-DEPTH MARKET INFORMATION and news, visit the Bloomberg website at **www.bloomberg.com**, which draws from the news and power of the BLOOMBERG PROFESSIONAL® service and Bloomberg's host of media products to provide high-quality news and information in multiple languages on stocks, bonds, currencies, and commodities.

About the Author

STEVE CONE is managing director and head of advertising and brand management at Citigroup Global Wealth Management. Along with five other senior executives, he coordinates worldwide brand management for all of Citigroup's businesses in more than 100 countries and encompassing 200 million customers. He also oversees advertising and brand management for The Citigroup Private Bank and Citigroup's Smith Barney businesses.

Prior to joining Citigroup, Cone was president of Fidelity's retail business and Fidelity's Chief Marketing Officer.

Cone is one of the most respected figures in financial services marketing. At Fidelity, he launched a successful advertising campaign featuring renowned former portfolio manager Peter Lynch, helping drive significant increases in the sale of Fidelity mutual funds. He also managed Fidelity's successful expansion into discount brokerage, making it the world's largest provider in that industry.

Over his thirty-year career—half of it in financial services—Cone has earned a reputation for innovative marketing management, with stops along the way at Key Corp, an earlier stint at Citibank, and seven years at American Express managing their branding strategy worldwide. In 1972, he graduated magna cum laude from Coe College with a degree in English literature.